GARDEN PESTS AND DISEASES
OF FLOWERS AND SHRUBS

GARDEN PESTS and DISEASES OF FLOWERS AND SHRUBS

Mogens Dahl and
Thyge B. Thygesen

English editor
A. M. Toms

Illustrations by
Verner Hancke

MACMILLAN PUBLISHING CO., INC.
NEW YORK

Macmillan Publishing Co., Inc.
866 Third Avenue, New York, N.Y. 10022

First American Edition 1974

Library of Congress Cataloging in Publication Data

Dahl, Mogens
    Garden pests and diseases of flowers and shrubs.
    Translation of Havens fjender i farver.
    Bibliography: p. 215
1. Garden pests. 2. Plants—Ornamental—Diseases and pests.
3. Pest Control. I. Thygesen, Thyge B., joint author. II. Title.
SB603.5.D3413   1974   635.9′2   74-8701
ISBN 0-02-619400-7

Color printed in Denmark by
F. E. Bording A/S, Copenhagen

Text printed in England by Fletcher & Son Ltd., Norwich
and bound by Richard Clay (The Chaucer Press) Ltd, Bungay, Suffolk

CONTENTS

INTRODUCTION

There are many books on gardening and most of them briefly mention pests and diseases in connection with some of the plants. A comprehensive book on the pests and diseases of the flower and ornamental bush and tree garden is unusual, but one with 313 colour illustrations is unique. Included are details of some physiological disorders and the methods by which nature exerts its own controlling influence, with notes on the methods of artificial control, including chemicals, that can be used to supplement nature's efforts when necessary.

Originally written in Danish by Mogens Dahl, a plant pathologist, and Thyge B. Thygesen, an entomologist, with illustrations by Verner Hancke, the English edition has been prepared by A. M. Toms, an independent consultant, with the assistance of his wife, Anna Marie, particularly with the translation.

An Appendix has been added to the original book to provide the reader with an outline of plant health regulations in several countries, and the regulations governing the sale and use of pesticides, together with a list of those products approved in the U.K. by the Agricultural Chemicals Approvals Scheme of the Ministry of Agriculture, Fisheries and Food and in common use in most other countries.

Most of the information provided in this book will be of value to gardeners throughout the world, except that the seasons, and therefore the times of infestations and infections, will differ according to the country.

DISEASES

There are two types of plant disease, (1) those that are caused by a pathological organism and are transmissible, and (2) those caused by physiological conditions where no pathological organism is involved and which are not transmitted from one plant to another. It is important that these two types are distinguished since control measures depend on correct diagnosis.

TRANSMISSIBLE DISEASES

These are essentially caused in plants by fungi, bacteria or viruses.

Fungus diseases

A fungus is basically a very primitive plant, consisting of thread-like cells only visible to the naked eye when in a mass. They are then known as mycelium. Reproduction is by spores which are only visible when magnified, being about 1/30 mm in length. The spores are sometimes formed at the end of the individual threads or mycelia, or develop in special growths called spore cases. Spore cases vary from being just visible with the naked eye to large specialised growths such as mushrooms. A few fungi produce hard, black bodies, several millimetres long, which can remain viable in the soil on dead plant tissue for six to ten years. These resting bodies are called sclerotia.

Fungi live either on living tissue, when they are parasitic, or on dead, decaying material when they are saprophytic. Fungi that cause disease are parasitic. They grow best under conditions of high humidity and temperature and when their host plant is growing poorly or has an excess of one nutrient.

Some fungi have a host change during the year, i.e. they have to live on more than one family or species of plant each year.

7

Others do not need an alternate host and even those needing one can, on occasion, survive without it.

Fungi can overwinter in a variety of sites: in the soil, on dead leaves, under bud scales or on live shoots and branches. Certain types can only attack one species of plant, e.g. Tulip Fire, *Botrytis tulipae*, while others, like the common grey mould, *Botrytis cinerea*, can attack hundreds of plant species.

There are various classifications of fungi, but for the gardener they can be divided roughly into the following principal types:

(1) **Soil dwelling fungi** grow into the roots, bulbs, corms and hypocotyl—the area between root and shoot in seedlings. They are therefore most damaging to seedlings, which have minimal resistance. Larger plants can also be considerably weakened since the supply of water and minerals to their leaves can be seriously impaired.

(2) **Branch fungi** can produce scars or cracks on branches, stems and shoots which cause ringing and strangulation. Wilting and death occur above the site of attack.

(3) **Leaf spot fungi** produce round spots of varying size, from a few millimetres to several centimetres in diameter. The spots are usually yellowish or yellow-green at first, but later become brown and black, often with a light grey centre. The black spore cases produced can often be seen under a magnifying glass.

(4) **Grey moulds** begin with the germination of a single spore which quickly develops into a small round spot of fungal growth. Under suitable conditions this spreads, and a grey-brown velvety cover appears with rapid decay of the plant tissue. If the humidity falls sufficiently the mould can cease and the decayed part will drop away, leaving a dry spot.

(5) **Rust fungi** can have up to four types of spore and two or more host changes which are essential for the disease to exist. Some rusts on conifers have these host changes. Because of the different types of spores there are differing symptoms, but the most common are brown-red, rust-coloured pustules.

(6) **Mildews** are produced by two basically different types of fungi, the powdery mildews and the downy mildews. Both,

however, principally attack young leaves and shoots and also flower stalks, bud bracts and sometimes the sepals. Powdery mildews produce a white covering, while the downy mildews can produce a greyish-white covering with the tissue underneath turning dark. With downy mildews, in particular, the attacked parts cease to grow and become deformed. The mildews differ from other fungi in respect of treatment, which also varies between the powdery and downy mildews.

Bacterial diseases

Like fungi, bacteria are types of simple plants. They are, however, so primitive that they consist of a single cell which is less than a thousandth of a millimetre in diameter. Multiplication is by cell division and can occur very rapidly. Not many plants are attacked by bacteria and chemical control is very difficult. There are three principal types of attack:

(1) **Rots** which attack the leaf, stems, bulbs and tubers where the diseased tissue becomes soft and often bad smelling. Decay quickly spreads, especially in humid, warm conditions.

(2) **Leaf spots** caused by bacteria are usually quite small and when held up to the light have a clear yellow edge.

(3) **Galls** can be on the roots, over the soil surface or on branches and shoots. They can measure a few millimetres to a couple of centimetres. They can also become attached to each other and form large knobs.

Fireblight (no. 67) has very special symptoms in which the leaf, flower, fruit and branches wilt and die.

Virus diseases

Virus diseases play an important role in the growth of ornamental plants, but it has only been in the last twenty to thirty years that their importance has been realised. Many growth disturbances previously thought to be degeneration are now known to be caused by viruses.

While fungi and bacteria are simple organisms, visible when magnified normally, virus particles are nucleo-proteins, so small that they can only be seen with the aid of an electron microscope magnifying up to hundreds of thousands of times. Virus particles vary in size and form according to type. Some plant viruses are round, others are straight rods, while others are thread-like and bent. The round ones are 20–30 mμ in diameter and others are 700–800 mμ long. (Mμ is a millimicron, i.e. one millionth of a millimetre.) When a plant is infected the virus particles multiply rapidly, using up the protein in the plant in the process. This causes a disturbance in the normal rhythm of plant nutrition and growth.

Some virus diseases are very severe and kill the plants, others are very mild and produce latent infections which do not show any symptoms. However, most of the diseases are between these two extremes. Development of the virus depends on the type of plant, while susceptibility to a specific virus varies from species to species and between varieties of the same species. Growth conditions, in particular temperature, can influence the reaction of plants and therefore the visible degree of attack. High temperatures usually weaken and mask the signs of disease. Heavy fertilising can also depress the symptoms, but there is no cure for the disease.

The early symptoms of virus infection show as a lightening of the colour of the leaf veins. This light colour can spread all along the veins, producing a condition known as **veinal chlorosis**. Alternatively, the veins can thicken, causing **leaf curl**. If the areas of light colour spread to the whole leaf, **mottle** is produced.

The so-called **mosaic** virus disease is one of the most common and is caused by many plant viruses. In plants suffering from mosaic the symptoms can assume various forms. A few or many leaves can be spotted with various shades of yellow and green, they can be curled, creased or deformed in other ways. The flowers can be spotted or streaked in various colours or otherwise deformed. **Necrosis**, which is brown dead streaks or circles, can also appear on the leaves, flower stems and flowers. Similar symptoms can appear on the growth from bulbs and corms.

Diseased plants are the most common vectors of these diseases.

Whether or not they show symptoms, the disease is all over an attacked plant in the sap stream.

Transmission can be by various methods:

(1) Seed transmission can occur, but this is not very common.

(2) Vegetative propagation, e.g. cuttings, grafting, bulbs and tubers, from infected plants transmits the virus.

(3) Transmission can also be caused by direct contact between infected and healthy plants, and through tools such as secateurs and pruning knives.

(4) The most common method of transmission is by insects, especially aphids, leaf hoppers, plant bugs, thrips and beetles. Nematodes (eelworms) have also been shown to act as vectors, and recent studies have also implicated fungi.

NON-TRANSMISSIBLE DISEASES
(Physiological disorders)

Physiological disorders are caused when certain parts of the plant system are malfunctioning. They can also be described as growth disturbances. Physiological disorders are not transmitted as they are not caused by parasites. Because there is no visible organism it is often difficult to determine the cause of poor growth. It is not possible to give all the physiological symptoms in a general book such as this, but the causes of these symptoms can be roughly divided into three groups: nutrient deficiency, climatic and scorching.

Nutrient deficiency—nourishment diseases

It can be said that the deficiency, or excess, of a nutrient will cause nourishment diseases. The nutrients available to a plant must be balanced and this is a science in itself. Usually the excess of a specific nutrient will not produce defined symptoms except in the case of some trace elements such as manganese, boron and copper. Excesses of such elements cause leaf distortion and die-back of the shoots. An excess of nitrogen produces a very vegetative, weak plant, rather prone to pathological diseases.

Deficiency diseases occur if the soil is inherently poor and unfertilised or if the roots are unable to absorb the nutrients present. This latter factor can be due to an excess of calcium, a lack of air or the formation of compounds unavailable to the plant.

Plants vary in their tolerance to lime, some will grow in acid soils, others must have alkaline conditions.

The illustrations, nos. 279–284, show only leaves suffering from a single nutrient deficiency.

Weather damage
Climatic conditions can cause various types of damage. High or low temperatures, hailstones, snow, drought or flooding are all responsible for plant damage. Frost damage occurs at a temperature of less than 0°C, and when the temperature is below the ideal for growing, particularly with a drying wind, cold damage is caused. Plants will also suffer if there are wide variations in temperature.

Excessive watering of plants causes the root system to be very shallow, so that wilting occurs much more readily during dry spells. Poor soil drainage causes waterlogging during rainy spells with stunted yellow growth. Drought can cause blindness of flower buds and a reduction in flower production.

Scorch and distortion
Scorch, i.e. when the leaves, buds and flowers become discoloured and the plants stop growing, can be caused by weather conditions and various chemicals. Wood preservatives splashed onto plants, or their vapour, can cause scorching as can certain weedkillers, such as sodium chlorate or paraquat. Drift from hormone weedkillers used on the lawn will cause leaf and stem distortion, sometimes serious enough to kill annuals and cause die-back on bushes and shrubs.

If fungicides and insecticides are not applied according to the instructions on the label and there is serious over-dosage or susceptible plants are sprayed, scorch can result. Sprays applied by aerosols can scorch by freezing if there is over-dosage or the nozzle is held too close to the plant. However phytotoxicity, producing scorch, from pesticides is not common.

Gases from industrial fumes will sometimes scorch seedlings but rarely harm older plants. If the causes of scorch or distortion are not obvious it is best to call in expert advice to avoid future trouble.

PESTS

Pests include all members of the animal kingdom, such as insects, mites, nematodes, molluscs, birds and both domestic and wild mammals.

Insects
The majority of insect species do no harm at all but play a general role in the balance of nature. A few are injurious to plant health, while a few are beneficial in that they are either parasitic or predatory on the harmful ones. Insects cause damage by either eating the plant tissue or sucking the juices and sap. They can also spread virus diseases without causing any visible mechanical damage. Both larvae and adults can live on plant tissue, and the damage caused can either be above or below ground.

Insect populations are dependent upon climatic conditions and the number of their natural enemies. It is, however, the natural enemies rather than the climatic conditions which produce the definite cycle of pest infestations. The natural enemies are insect parasites and predators, animal predators, fungus and virus parasites. Together in a natural environment they can keep insect pest populations under control, but gardens are really artificial environments, both in respect of plants and insect pests.

Mites
Insects have six legs and antennae, while mites have eight legs and no antennae. The mites causing plant damage are

0·1–0·5 mm long and can only just be seen with the naked eye.

Spider mites can become serious pests because they have a very short life cycle and a rapid rate of reproduction, so that very large populations can build up quickly under favourable conditions.

Leaf-feeding mites suck the plant juices so that the leaves turn yellow and die, starved by a loss of chlorophyll. The gall mites cause the plants to produce an abnormal number of cells where they feed so that galls are formed, inside which the mites live protected from their natural enemies. Normal plant growth is inhibited and even stopped, but the plants are not killed, for this would be to the disadvantage of the mites.

There are a very large number of species of spider mites both above and below ground, but most are harmless and few show their presence. The leaf gall mites are very visible, yet only slightly affect plant growth. Gall mites are very specific in respect of host plants and will normally only attack one plant species.

Nematodes

These are commonly called eelworms and are very small round worms. They have various methods of living, some are parasitic on living plants, some on decaying vegetable material, some are parasitic on insects and other forms of animal life in the soil, while others are completely free living.

Although the parasitic plant eelworms can attack the leaf, flower stalk or roots, each species is site specific. Many species form cysts, i.e. the female forms a hard skin around herself which contains eggs and larvae and this remains viable for years, contaminating host crops whenever they are grown.

Molluscs

These are slugs and snails, slugs being naked or shell-less snails. There are large numbers of both slugs and snails in gardens and they vary greatly in size and the damage they do, many living chiefly on decaying vegetable matter in the soil. Snails tend to scrape leaves, shoots and flowers, while slugs eat the plants. Their natural enemies are many birds, and also frogs and toads.

Gnawing mammals

Many wild mammals will cause damage by gnawing the bark or roots of trees and shrubs. Field mice, voles, rabbits and hares damage the stems, while moles and rats attack the roots. Moles are also a nuisance, tunnelling and throwing up heaps of soil on lawns and moving the roots of plants in borders.

Dogs and cats

Domestic animals are really just a nuisance, particularly when they belong to a neighbour. Urination by dogs can cause scorching on the lawn and on herbaceous plants. Cats digging for toilet purposes among seedlings can be annoying.

Birds

Some birds cause damage, but others are beneficial. Starlings will make holes in lawns searching for insect larvae and ants, and larger birds occasionally appear in country gardens in search of cockchafer grubs and leatherjackets. While causing some damage, their activities are also beneficial. Sparrows will often peck crocus flowers to pieces, and, once they get into this habit, will damage other plants in the same way. Other birds, particularly bullfinches, can strip ornamental bushes and trees of flower buds. Woodpeckers can sometimes be seen searching under the bark of older trees for insect larvae.

Much of the damage done by birds in gardens is caused by their mischievousness and not by their feeding habits, which in the main are beneficial. On balance they should be welcomed and not driven away.

CONTROL MEASURES AND METHODS

The illustrations and text in this book should enable gardeners to identify most of the pests and diseases of ornamental plants in their gardens. Some gardeners attempt to eliminate pests and diseases, while others prevent the worst damage occurring and maintain a fairly natural equilibrium. In all cases prevention is better than cure, and by adopting sound principles much of the damage caused by pests and diseases can be prevented or minimised, thus avoiding the unnecessary use of chemicals.

Phytosanitation

This is basically plant cleanliness and involves the removal and burning of all diseased or decaying plant material whether still on the plant or on the ground. One of the principle sources of infection is decaying, diseased material left lying around in the garden during the winter. Diseased plant material should not be composted, but must be burnt immediately to prevent the spread of infection.

Crop rotation

Annual plants should not always be grown in the same place in the garden. Moving them assists in reducing the incidence of pests and diseases and in maintaining the condition of the soil. Perennials, bushes and shrubs cannot be rotated and therefore must be continually cleaned of diseases or decaying material and the soil well maintained.

Soil improvement

A well growing, healthy plant is not easily damaged by pests and diseases. To achieve healthy plants, the soil's physical and chemical condition must be maintained correctly for the plants growing in it. The soil must be porous for aeration and root growth, and the nutrients present in their correct proportions.

Buried compost assists the physical condition of the soil, particularly heavy and clay soils, and provides a source of balanced, slowly released plant nutrients. Artificial fertilisers should always be used as supplements, regularly and often and according to the instructions of the manufacturer. They must never be over-applied at any one time.

Resistant species and varieties

Many wild species of plants are completely resistant, even immune, to attacks from certain pests and diseases, even when climatic conditions are suitable for attack. In producing more attractive plants for the garden plant breeders have made many varieties more susceptible to disease and pest attack, but they are now using inherited resistance to improve new varieties in this respect. Catalogues usually contain information on the susceptibility or resistance of varieties to certain pests and diseases, e.g. mildew on roses, and wherever possible resistant or immune varieties should be grown.

Plants are resistant when they can be attacked but suffer no actual damage. Immunity means that it is impossible for them to be attacked, a characteristic much more difficult to breed into them than resistance. There are occasions when individual plants within a variety or species show resistance to a pest or disease, and these should be selected for future propagation. This is plant selection and not plant breeding for resistance.

Plant health regulations

Legislation concerning plant health varies between countries, but it is usually concerned with specific diseases and pests rather than with plant health in general, for example, the Fireblight Order at present operative in the U.K. and the Orders concerning Dutch Elm Disease operative in several countries. Plant Quarantine Regulations strictly control the import of plants and bulbs all over the world. They are designed to prevent undesirable insects and diseases from entering countries where they are not present or have been eradicated, e.g. Colorado Beetle into the U.K., Mediterranean Fruit Fly into the U.S.A.

Some countries, such as the U.S.A., have regular inspections of plant nurseries to make certain that the stock is free of obnoxious pests and diseases and is healthy. In most countries it has been found difficult to administer laws which endeavour to ensure that only healthy plants and plant material are distributed. A system of voluntary certification of stocks is operated in some countries for certain plants, but this usually applies to fruit and vegetables and not to ornamentals.

Plant health regulations are enforceable in respect of the movement of plants between countries, but within a country they are only as good as the co-operation of the general public makes them. Gardeners should always make certain that they are purchasing healthy, disease-free plants. This is not always easy, but it is hoped that the illustrations and text in this book will enable any gardener to inspect plant nurseries during the growing season and decide for themselves whether the stock is disease-free and that pests are kept under control. Only if nurseries conforming to plant health regulations and maintaining a high standard of phytosanitation and pest and disease control are patronised, will the standard of nursery stock be maintained at a high level.

Treatment

The preventive measures already discussed assist plants to resist the attack of pests and disease, but it is still possible for plants to be damaged unless treated. Biological control (see p. 22) cannot be undertaken by the gardener, but every endeavour should be made to utilise those beneficial insects, animals, etc., present in the garden. These, together with preventive measures and chemicals, can form a system of integrated control (see p. 21).

In the early stages of a disease, pruning and burning the diseased tissue will often prevent the spread of the disease. Pests should only be treated with chemicals in the early stages of an attack if climatic and other conditions are favourable to the pest. When chemicals are used it must always be in accordance with the instructions on the label. Excessive dosages must never be applied.

It should be remembered that most fungicides are preventive or prophylactic and do not cure diseases, while insecticides are designed to rapidly kill the pest.

Pesticide regulations

These vary considerably between countries but a summary of some of them is given in the Appendix.

Labelling of pesticides

Since gardeners use only small quantities of pesticides they are supplied in small packs, and this means that the labels are small. Sometimes a supplementary label is tied onto the pack, in addition to the one printed or stuck on. These labels must all be read if the product is to be used properly.

The label, in addition to the precautions to be taken, the active ingredient, and the use to which it should be put, will also give clear instructions in respect of dilution rates and quantities, and the plants that can be treated. It will also state whether it can be mixed with other chemicals to provide, for example, a combined insecticide and fungicide.

Storage is important with all chemicals in order to avoid accidents. It is always clearly stated under the heading of 'Precautions' on the label how the product should be stored, but it is important always to store any chemical in its original labelled container, tightly closed and in a safe place, preferably in a locked cupboard in the tool shed.

Providing chemicals are used in accordance with the precautions and instructions on the label, they are not dangerous and will not cause pollution of the environment. No laws regulating the manufacture, sale and use of chemicals can prevent misuse by those who will not obey the instructions on the label, and gardeners must remember that they are as much a part of the schemes or regulations as are governments and the chemical industry.

Treatments and application methods

(a) **Fungicides.** There are various commercial preparations for specific purposes. Some active ingredients and the diseases they control are given in the Appendix but there are probably others available in certain markets which are equally effective. The commercial preparations are at varying strengths and the correct dilution rates are given on the individual labels.

(b) **Insecticides.** These are similar to fungicides in respect of their formulation and labelling. A list of many of those available to gardeners, with their specific uses, is given in the Appendix.

(c) **Bacteriacides.** Really suitable chemicals against bacteria have not yet been produced in spite of considerable research. Restrictions on the antibiotics used in human medicine have made research more difficult. Phytosanitation, together with the use of certain fungicides, such as those based on copper compounds, is the most effective treatment so far.

(d) **Wound sealants.** These products have various bases, but to be really effective they should also contain a fungicide to prevent fungus spores entering through the wound.

(e) **Treatment of virus diseases.** In a garden the cure of virus diseases is impossible. In research and plant breeding stations virus free plants are produced by either heat treatment or meristem culture, i.e. the culture of microscopic growth points in artificial media in a test tube.

The most practical methods of virus control are: (1) the use of healthy plant material; (2) the control of insects and other vectors; (3) placing healthy material well away from any source of infection and (4) immediate removal of attacked plants where economic and practical.

(f) **Repellents.** These are required to prevent damage from birds and mammals, both wild and domestic. There are no approved repellents in the U.K. as none act satisfactorily all the time, and their effectiveness is most difficult to prove. They must be harmless yet make the plants unpleasant by smell or taste.

(g) **Dusting.** Dusts are supplied already formulated for immediate application without further mixing. Over-dosing with a dust must be avoided. Treated plants should not be covered with an obvious layer of powder, otherwise the leaves will not function properly and cannot obtain nutrients from the air. The amount of powder is correct when it is only just visible. Quantities for a given area are irrelevant for garden use as it is not specific areas that are treated, but individual plants.

(h) **Spraying.** There are two types of formulation available for spraying, apart from those ready to apply. These are emulsifiable concentrates, which are liquids and can be added directly to the water, or powders which must be creamed into a very thin paste with a little liquid before being added to the water in the spraying apparatus. In both cases it is preferable to half fill the sprayer with water, add the chemical and then complete the filling, stirring before beginning to spray.

Full directions for dilution are on the label and these must be followed. Spraying and dusting is preferably done in the morning and evening and not in very hot weather in the middle of the day. Also the wind should not be too strong, otherwise the wrong plants will be sprayed, but this is more important with weed-killers. Wherever possible open flowers should not be sprayed when the precautions on the label state that there is a danger to bees.

Some ready to spray pesticides are made up in the form of aerosols. It must be remembered that the propellant used in aerosols can cause frost damage if the aerosol is held too close to the plant when spraying. As with all other chemicals, the instructions on the label must be read and followed carefully.

Pollution and contamination

The use of chemicals by gardeners contributes very little to the pollution of the environment, particularly now that certain compounds are no longer available in the small packages. If the pesticides currently available to gardeners are used correctly and according to instructions, there is no risk of pollution.

There are risks of accidental contamination of such things as fish ponds, some of the natural insecticides, for example derris, are lethal to fish in very small quantities. Disposal of the empty package must be in accordance with the instruction on the label to avoid accidental contamination.

No chemical, whether a pesticide, medicine or food, is non-poisonous when used carelessly or in excess. Some pesticides are safer than many chemicals in daily use in this respect, and millions of pounds are spent annually in research for new pesticides.

Integrated pest and disease control, including biological control methods

Unfortunately, when a garden is made the balance of nature in that small area is completely upset, because plants not previously part of the biological environment are introduced. Gardeners also wish that these plants should be as picturesque as possible and grow healthily. They are, however, more susceptible to many pests and diseases than those growing in a wild state, which have often selected themselves for resistance and can tolerate and live in harmony with their natural enemies.

Keen gardeners are also lovers of nature, and it is in their own interests that they should study to some degree the natural methods of pest and disease control so that they can integrate these with chemical methods to produce healthy, beautiful plants.

Biological control consists of utilising and, if possible, harnessing the natural enemies of the plant pests so that the pests are kept in check and under control. This works most satisfactorily in controlled environments where the pest and parasite/predator relationship can be regulated, such as in glasshouses for the control of the Red Spider Mite, *Tetranychus urticae*, with a predator mite, *Phytoseiulus persimilis*. In outdoor situations the parasite/predator of a pest reduces the pest population so that it has insufficient food and then itself is so reduced in numbers that the pest becomes dominant again.

A further difficulty in respect of biological control for the gardener is the time lag between a fairly high pest population and its control by parasites/predators. Large scale release of parasites/predators does not alleviate this situation unless it is done as the pest population is just starting to increase. Illustrations nos. 296–313 show some of the creatures useful to gardeners, and if some of these, particularly ladybirds and their larvae, hover fly larvae and lacewing larvae, are present in large numbers among an infestation of aphids, chemicals need not, and should not, be used.

Over large areas the release of insect parasites and predators have, on occasions, produced spectacular results with a natural balance being eventually reached so that the pest ceases to be one. The use of the parasitic bacteria, *Bacillus thuringiensis*, has been only partially successful commercially since the spores are produced artificially, stored and then sprayed. It is specific to the caterpillars of butterflies and moths which have to eat sprayed leaves. The bacteria build up in the caterpillars and produce toxins which kill them after a few days. The time lag is often too great for this method to be likely to replace chemical insecticides which kill the pest in a few hours.

Other parasitic micro-organisms, including the polyhedral viruses, are being intensively studied throughout the world as methods of biological control, but progress is slow due to the dangers of mutation and that some may become harmful to human life. One serious garden pest in the U.S.A., the Japanese Beetle, is being successfully controlled by spraying a fungus onto the overwintering larvae in the soil, but such successes are rather uncommon.

A semi-biological control technique, with some successful applications, has been the release of artificially bred males of a pest previously sterilised by radio-activity or chemosterilants. This is really successful only when the female of the pest mates once, and lays only one batch of eggs which will be unfertilised.

However, these various methods of biological control only form part of integrated pest and disease control. All techniques, including good growing conditions, phytosanitation, biological control and the correct use of chemicals should be combined to produce the most natural and efficient method of pest and disease control.

1. Fir rust, *Pucciniastrum pustulatum* **2.** Damage by night frost **3.** Transplanting damage on Noble Fir, *Abies nobilis* **4.** Silver Fir adelges, *Dreyfusia nordmannianae*

5

5 b

5 a

6

7 a

5. Attack by green pineapple gall aphid, *Sacci-phantes viridis*, **a.** dried-up gall, **b.** section through gall **6.** Winter damage **7.** Douglas Fir aphid, *Gilletteella cooleyi*, **a.** dried-up gall **8.** Attack by strawberry-gall aphid, *Adelges tardus*, **a.** dried-up gall **9.** Damage by Sitka spruce aphid, *Neomyzaphis abietina*

10a

10

12

10. Vapourer moth caterpillars, *Orgyia antiqua*,
a. enlarged **11.** Death of buds caused by the
fungus *Cucurbitaria piceae*, **a.** enlarged **12.**
Damage caused by the caterpillars of the
Spruce needle roller moth, *Eucosma tedella*
13. Conifer spider mite, *Oligonychus ununguis*, on
Dwarf Spruce, *Picea glauca* 'Cornica', **a.** Enlarged **b.** on Norway Spruce, *Picea abies*

14   14a   14b

15

15a

16a

14. Nun moth, *Lymantria monacha*, **a.** pupa **b.** caterpillar **15.** Large bark beetle, *Dendroctonus micans*, **a.** larval tunnels **16.** Typograph bark beetle, *Ips typographus*, enlarged, **a.** larval tunnels **17.** Root disease, *Fomes annosus* **18.** Stem strangulation by Honeysuckle, *Lonicera periclymenum*

19   20

22

Pine (*Pinus*)

21

22 a

19. Pine bark blister rust, *Cronartium ribicola*, on two-needled pine **20.** Needleless parts of a branch after the male flowers **21.** Pine bark blister rust, *Cronartium pini*, on five-needled pine **22.** Pine needle blister rust, *Coleosporium pini*, **a.** on Groundsel, *Senecio vulgaris*

23. Fungus disease, *Scleroderris lagerbergii*, drying out buds and branches, **a.** old damage **24.** Winter damage **25.** Hare damage on pine needles

24

25

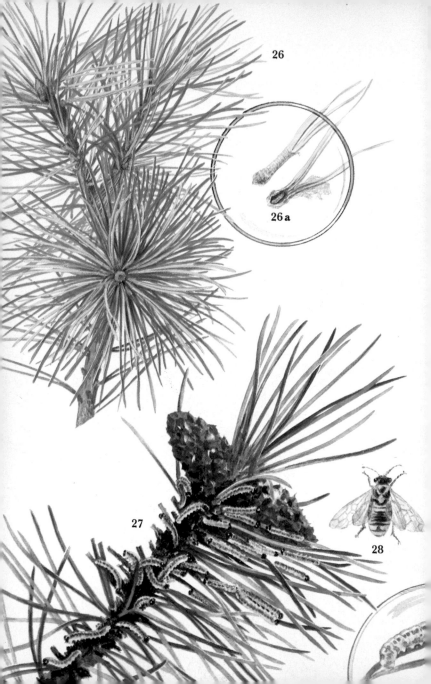

26

26 a

27

28

26. Damage by the Pine needle sheath gall midge, *Thecodiplosis brachyntera*, **a.** needle sheaths with larva **27.** Attack by caterpillars of the Pine sawfly, *Lophyrus pini*, **a.** larva enlarged **28.** Pine sawfly, *Lophyrus pini*, female, **a.** male **29.** Woodpecker damage on pine cone **30.** Pine-shoot moth, *Evetria buoliana*, caterpillars damaging young shoots, **a.** larva **b.** moth, both enlarged **31.** Pine stem aphid, *Pineus pini*, **a.** enlarged

32. Needle drop disease, *Meria laricis* **33.** Larch canker, *Dasyscypha willkommii* **34.** Green pine-apple gall aphid, *Sacchiphantes viridis*, **a.** on Spruce **35.** Roe deer horn rubbing

Larch (*Larix*)

34

34 a

35

36
36a
37
37a

36. Larch needle miner, *Coleophora laricinella*, **a.** larva enlarged **37.** Larch cone eaten by the cone borer moth, *Dioryctria abietella*, **a.** section of damaged cone enlarged **38.** Damage by the Spruce spinning mite, *Oligonychus ununguis*, on Juniper, **a.** healthy branch **39.** Damage by Juniper moth, *Nothris marginella*, caterpillars

40

40a

41

41a

41b

42

43

40. Winter damage, light and severe, **a.** healthy branch **41.** Juniper tongue rust, *Gymnosporangium clavariaeforme*, **a.** in dry weather **b.** in damp weather, both enlarged **42.** Branch death, *Phomopsis juniperovora* or *Kabatina juniperi* **43.** Juniper gall rust, *Gymnosporangium sabinae*

44

44 a

45 a

45

47

47a

46

44. Leaf aphid, *Lachniella sp.*, **a.** enlarged **45.** Thuja scale, *Eulecanium arion*, **a.** enlarged **46.** Abnormal growth caused by poor soil conditions **47.** Thuja leaf spot disease, *Didymascella thujina*, **a.** enlarged

Yew (*Taxus*)

48

48 a

50

48. Damage by bark weevil, *Otiorrhynchus sulcatus*, **a.** chewing, enlarged **49.** Yew scale, *Eulecanium crudum*, **a.** enlarged **50.** Frost damage **51.** Gall mite, *Eriophyes psilaspis*, **a.** enlarged

52. Damage by Box gall midge, *Monarthropalpus buxi*, **a.** enlarged **53.** Damage by Box leaf sucker, *Psylla buxi* **54.** Mahonia rust, *Cumminsiella sanguinea*, **a.** under-surface of leaf **55.** Winter damage of Mahonia **56.** Damage by Holly leaf miner, *Phytomyza ilicis*, **a.** pupa, enlarged

54a

56a

56

55

57 b

58

58 a

57 a

57

57. Honey fungus, *Armillaria mellea*, **a.** fungus mycelium **b.** rhizomorphes 58. Douglas fir aphid, *Gilletteella cooleyi*, **a.** young shoot **b.** enlarged 59. Frost damage on Japanese Cedar, *Cryptomeria* 60. Variegation in *Thujopsis dolobrata*

Privet (*Ligustrum*)

61

62

64

61a

63

09 a

64 a

61. Privet hawk moth, *Sphinx ligustri*, **a.** caterpillar **62.** Attack by Tortrix moth, *Cacoecia rosana* **63.** Leaf aphid, *Aphis ligustri*, **a.** enlarged **64.** Attack by the Lilac moth, *Gracillaria syringella*, on Privet (*Ligustrum*), **a.** on Lilac (*Syringa*)

65

66

66 a

70 a

70

65. Thorn powdery mildew, *Podosphaera oxyacanthae*
66. Thorn aphid, *Ovatus crataegarius*, **a.** enlarged **67.** Fire-blight, *Erwinia amylovora* **68.** Thorn rose caused by the gall midge, *Dasyneura crataegi* **69.** Leaf sucker, *Psylla pyrisuga*, **a.** enlarged **70.** Thorn rust, *Gymnosporangium clavariaeforme*, **a.** on the berries

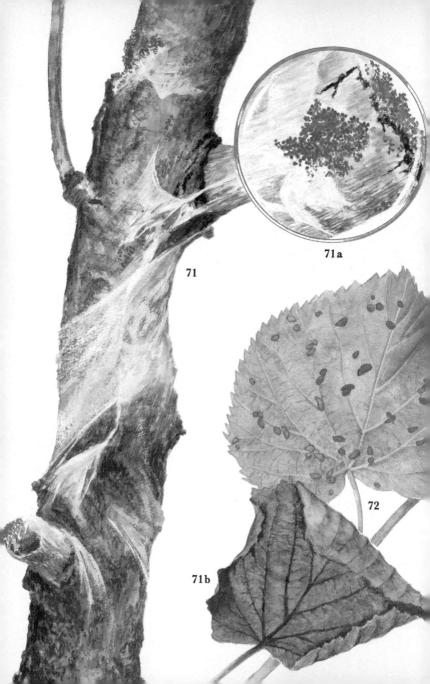

71

71a

71b

72

Lime (*Tilia*)

71. Attack by Lime red spider mite, *Tetranychus tiliae*, **a.** enlarged **b.** attacked leaf **72.** Attack by Lime gall mite, *Eriophyes tetratrichus* **73.** Horn-like galls produced by the mite, *Eriophyes tiliae* **74.** Mite felt produced by *Eriophyes liosoma*

75. Larva of leaf wasp, *Eriocampoides annulipes* **76.** San
José oyster-shell scale, *Quadraspidiotus perniciosus,* **a.** enlarged **77.** Birch leaf roller, *Deporaus betulae,* **a.** enlarged
78. Silver green-leaf weevil, *Phyllobius argentatus,* **a.** enlarged

Birch (*Betula*)

77 a

77

78 a

78

79. Witches broom, *Taphrina betulina* **80.** Attack by leaf miner, *Agromyza alni-betulae* **81.** Leaf aphid, *Euceraphis punctipennis*, **a.** enlarged **82.** Birch looper moth, *Biston betularius*, light and dark variant, **a.** caterpillar **83.** Birch rust, *Melampsoridium betulinum* **84.** Attack by gall mite, *Eriophyes brevitarsus*, **a.** enlarged **85.** Buff-tip moth, *Phalera bucephala*, **a.** caterpillar

Betula

81

81a

82

82a

84

84a

85

85a

86

87a

87

88

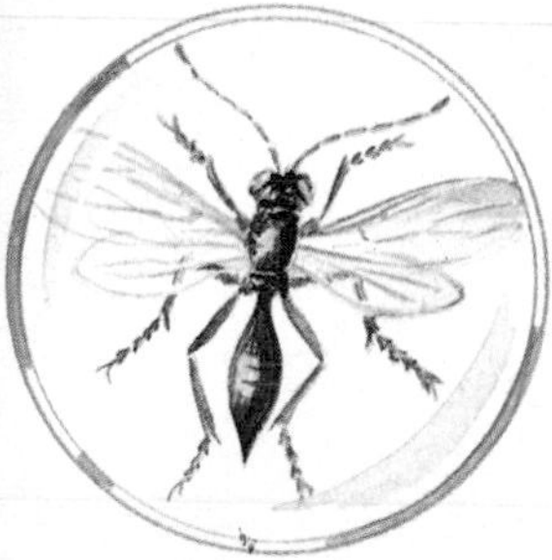

87b

86. Leaf galls produced by the gall wasp, *Diplolepis longiventris* **87.** Gall apples produced by the Oak gall wasp, *Diplolepis quercus-folii*, **a.** section of gall, with larva, enlarged, **b.** gall wasp, enlarged **88.** Disc galls produced by the gall wasp, *Neuroterus albipes* **89.** Oak powdery mildew, *Microsphaera quercina* **90.** Leaf spot, *Gloeosporium umbrinellum*, **a.** enlarged, **b.** lower surface of leaf

89

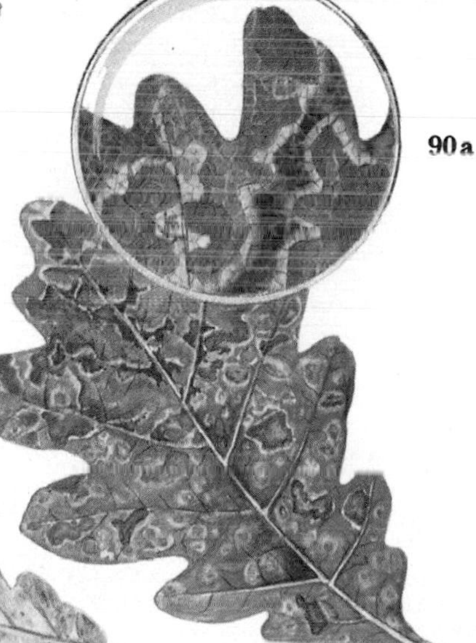

90a

90

90b

Elm (*Ulmus*)

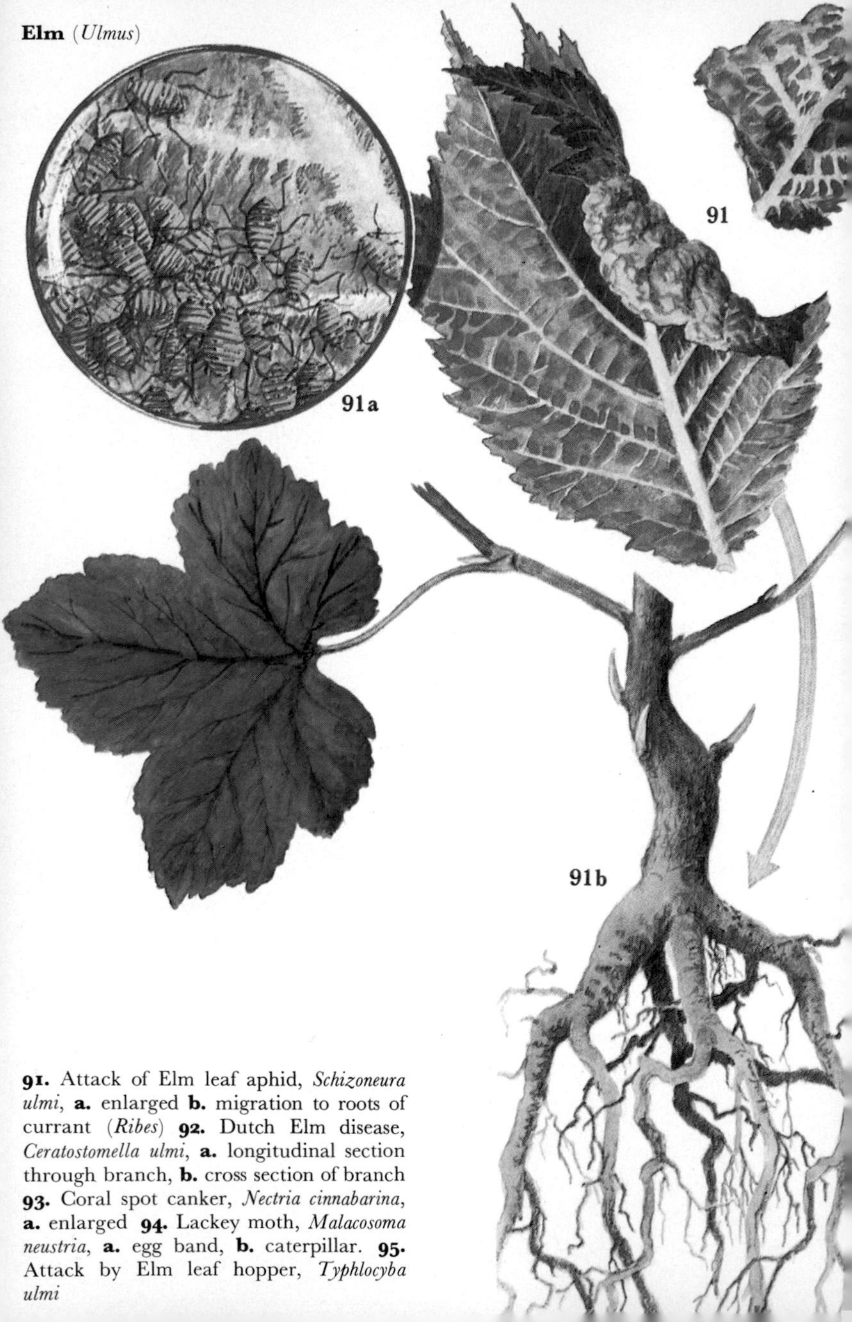

91a

91

91b

91. Attack of Elm leaf aphid, *Schizoneura ulmi*, **a.** enlarged **b.** migration to roots of currant (*Ribes*) **92.** Dutch Elm disease, *Ceratostomella ulmi*, **a.** longitudinal section through branch, **b.** cross section of branch **93.** Coral spot canker, *Nectria cinnabarina*, **a.** enlarged **94.** Lackey moth, *Malacosoma neustria*, **a.** egg band, **b.** caterpillar. **95.** Attack by Elm leaf hopper, *Typhlocyba ulmi*

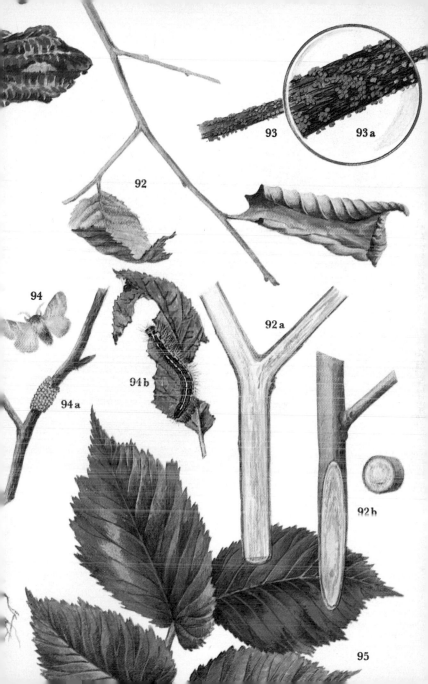

92

92 a

92 b

93

93 a

94

94 a

94 b

95

Beech (*Fagus*)

96

97

98

101   101a   101b

96. Beech scale, *Cryptococcus fagi* **97.** Gall produced by Beech gall midge, *Hartigiola annulipes* **98.** Gall produced by the gall midge *Mikiola fagi* **99.** Leaf 'felting' by the gall mite *Eriophyes nervisequus* **100.** Leaf 'felting' by a gall mite, *Eriophyes sp.* **101.** Attack by Beech leaf miner, *Orchestes fagi*, **a.** leaf holes eaten by weevil, **b.** leaf mines by larva **102.** Beech aphid, *Phyllaphis fagi*, **a.** enlarged

99

100

102 a

102

103

104 a

105

105 a

104

106

106 a

106 b

103. Gall midge, *Helicomyia saliciperda.* **104.** Leaf beetle, *Phyllodecta vulgatissima*, **a.** enlarged **105.** Gall produced by leaf wasp, *Pteronus salicis*, **a.** leaf wasp, enlarged **106.** Leopard moth, *Zeuzera pyrina*, larva, **a.** female, **b.** male

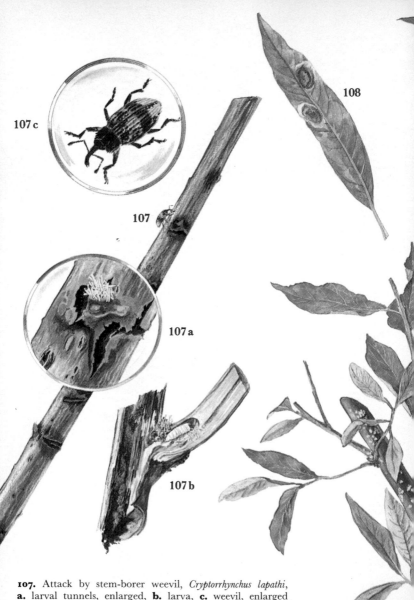

107. Attack by stem-borer weevil, *Cryptorrhynchus lapathi*, **a.** larval tunnels, enlarged, **b.** larva, **c.** weevil, enlarged **108.** Gall produced by the gall wasp *Pontania capreae* **109.** Willow mildew, *Uncinula salicis* **110.** Willow scale, *Chionaspis salicis*, **a.** enlarged **111.** Rust, *Melampsora spp.*, **a.** upper surface of leaf.

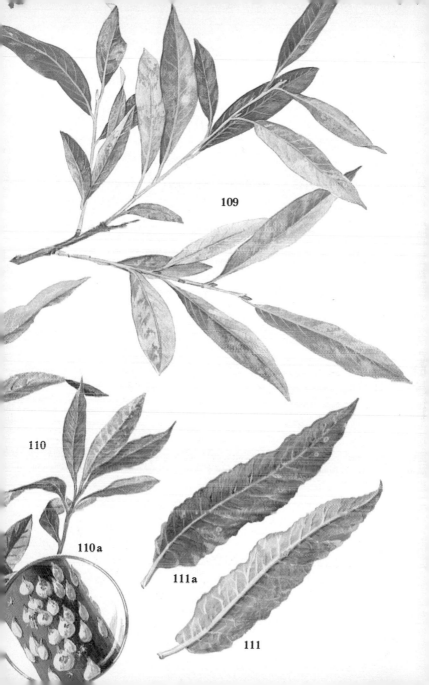

109

110

110a

111a

111

112

112. Willow scab, *Fusicladium saliciperdum*
113. Poplar scab, *Fusicladium radiosum* **114.**
Mosaic virus disease **115.** Poplar canker,
Dothichiza populea

Poplar (*Populus*)

113

114

115

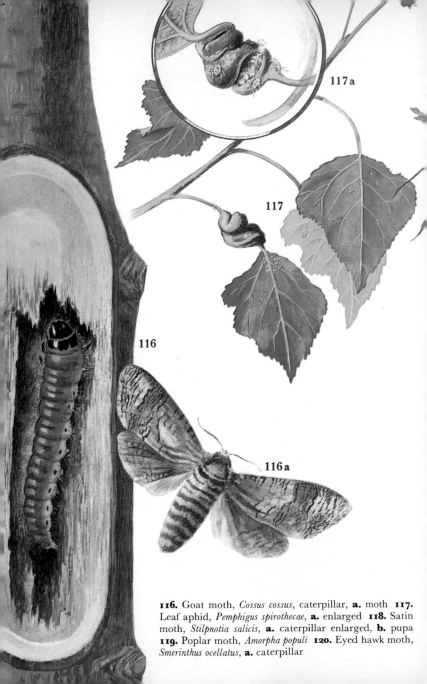

116. Goat moth, *Cossus cossus*, caterpillar, **a.** moth **117.** Leaf aphid, *Pemphigus spirothecae*, **a.** enlarged **118.** Satin moth, *Stilpnotia salicis*, **a.** caterpillar enlarged, **b.** pupa **119.** Poplar moth, *Amorpha populi* **120.** Eyed hawk moth, *Smerinthus ocellatus*, **a.** caterpillar

118

118 a

118 b

119

120 a

120

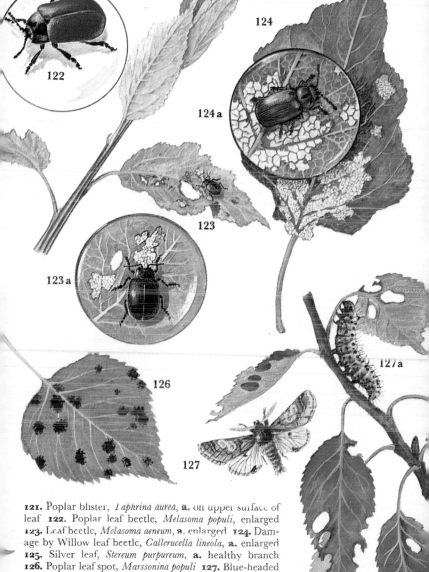

121. Poplar blister, *Taphrina aurea*, **a.** on upper surface of leaf **122.** Poplar leaf beetle, *Melasoma populi*, enlarged **123.** Leaf beetle, *Melasoma aeneum*, **a.** enlarged **124.** Damage by Willow leaf beetle, *Gallerucella lineola*, **a.** enlarged **125.** Silver leaf, *Stereum purpureum*, **a.** healthy branch **126.** Poplar leaf spot, *Marssonina populi* **127.** Blue-headed owl moth, *Episema coeruleocephala*, **a.** caterpillar

Sorbus

128 a

128

129

130

128. Rowan rust, *Gymnosporangium corniferum*, **a.** enlarged
129. Attack by gall mite, *Eriophyes goniothorax sorbeus*
130. Rowan mosaic virus disease **131.** Tar spot disease,
Rhytisma acerinum **132.** Attack of gall mite, *Eriophyes macrochelus*, **a.** on lower surface of leaf **133.** Mildew,
Uncinula circinata, on Hedge Maple (*Acer campestre*)

134

135

136a

136

137

134. Natural white and red variegation on Kolomikta Vine
(*Actinidia kolomikta*) **135.** Red currant blister aphid, *Cryptomyzus
ribis*, on Flowering Currant (*Ribes*) **136.** Physiological distortion of
branch (fasciation), **a.** healthy branch **137.** Bunching bacterial
disease, *Corynebacterium fascians*

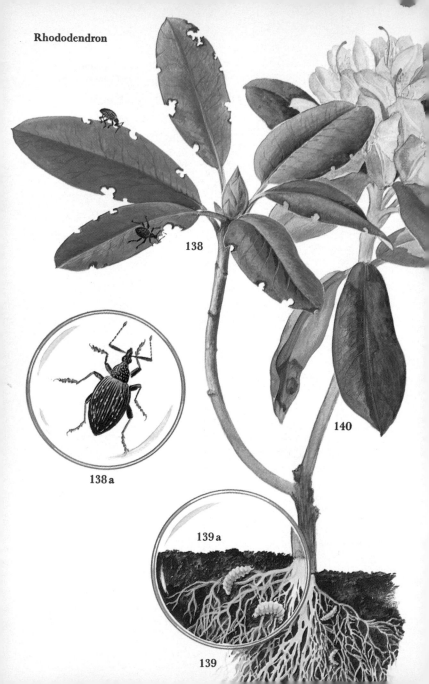

Rhododendron

138

138 a

139 a

139

140

141b

141

141a

142

142 a

138. Vine weevil, *Otiorrhynchus sulcatus*, **a.** enlarged **139.** Attack on roots by larvae of the Vine weevil, **a.** enlarged **140.** Winter damage **141.** Rhododendron bug, *Stephanitis rhododendri*, **a.** enlarged **b.** upper surface of leaf **142.** Rhododendron whitefly, *Dialeurodes chittendeni*, **a.** enlarged

Rhododendron and Heather (*Erica*)

143

144

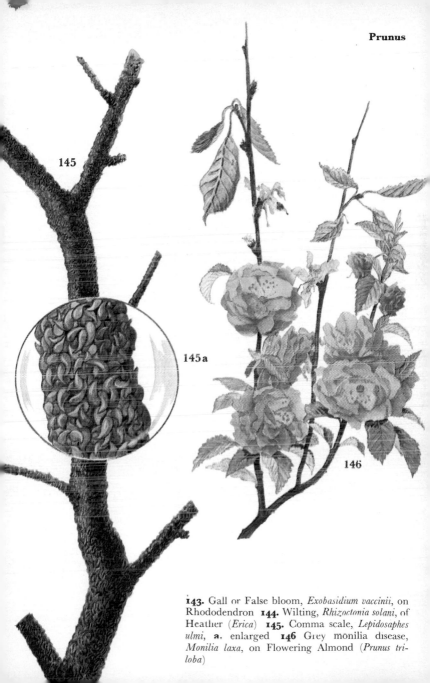

143. Gall or False bloom, *Exobasidium vaccinii*, on Rhododendron **144.** Wilting, *Rhizoctonia solani*, of Heather (*Erica*) **145.** Comma scale, *Lepidosaphes ulmi*, **a.** enlarged **146** Grey monilia disease, *Monilia laxa*, on Flowering Almond (*Prunus triloba*)

147a

147b

147

149

150

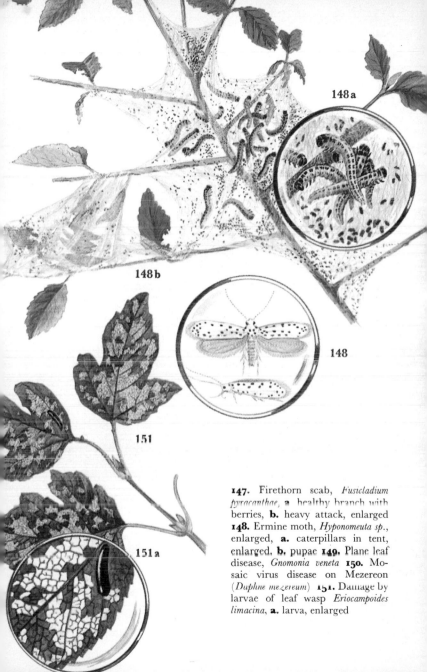

147. Firethorn scab, *Fusicladium pyracanthae*, **a.** healthy branch with berries, **b.** heavy attack, enlarged **148.** Ermine moth, *Hyponomeuta sp.*, enlarged, **a.** caterpillars in tent, enlarged, **b.** pupae **149.** Plane leaf disease, *Gnomonia veneta* **150.** Mosaic virus disease on Mezereon (*Daphne mezereum*) **151.** Damage by larvae of leaf wasp *Eriocampoides limacina*, **a.** larva, enlarged

152. Hare damage **153.** Attack of scale insect *Parthenolecanium coryli*, **a.** enlarged **154.** Wild oat rust, *Puccinia arrhenateri*, **a.** damaged flower cluster **b.** enlarged **155.** Black rust, *Puccinia graminis*, **a.** enlarged

153

153 a

152

154

155

154 b

154 a

155 a

156

157

156. Earwigs, *Forficula auricularia* 157. Powdery mildew, *Erysiphe polygoni* 158. Attack by Feather moth, *Orneodes hexadactyla* 159. Larval tunnels of the leaf miner, *Phytagromyza hendeliana*

160. Yellow mosaic virus disease on two different rose varieties **161.** Leaf-cutting bee, *Megachile centuncularis*, **a.** damaged leaves **162.** Powdery mildew of roses, *Sphaerotheca pannosa* **163.** Attack of Rose tortrix moth, *Cacoecia rosana*, **a.** moth and caterpillar, enlarged **164.** Attack by the Small rose-leaf wasp, *Blennocampa pusilla* **165.** Attack by the Rose-hip fly, *Spilographa alternata*, **a.** larva in the rose-hip.

Rose (*Rosa*)

161 a

161

164

163 a

165

165 a

166

166 a

166 b

168

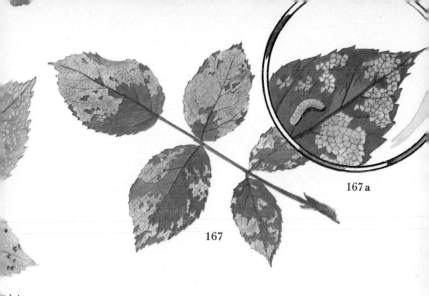

167a

167

170

166. Rose rust, *Phragmidium mucronatum*, **a.** lower surface of leaf, **b.** upper surface of leaf **167.** Damage by the Leaf wasp, *Eriocampoides aethiops*, **a.** skeletonising larva, enlarged **168.** Black spot of roses, *Diplocarpon rosae* **169.** Rose root gall, *Agrobacterium tumefaciens* **170.** Leaf damage by the Garden chafer, *Phyllopertha horticola*

169

171

172

174a

174

174b

171. Rose aphid, *Macrosiphum rosae*
172. Cold weather damage **173.** Abnormal growth caused by the gall wasp, *Rhodites rosae* **174.** Attack by the Rose leaf hopper, *Typhlocyba rosae*, **a.** lower surface of leaf, **b.** enlarged **175.** Rose stem with larva of the borer, *Ardis bipunctata*

176. Cold damage on *Rosa hugonis* **177.** Leaf crinkling by feeding of the capsid bug, *Lygus pabulinus* **178.** Leaf shot-hole disease, *Stigmina carpophila* **179.** Leaf scorch in spring

176

177

178

179

Cockchafer

180

181

180 g

180 a

180 f

180 b

180 c

180 d

180 e

180. Cockchafer, *Melolontha melolontha*, **a.** egg-laying female, **b.** first year larva, **c.** second year larva, **d.** third year larva, **e.** pupa, **f.** emerging adult, **g.** flying beetle **181.** Summer Chafer beetle, *Rhizotrogus solstitialis*, **a.** larva **182.** Garden Chafer beetle, *Phyllopertha horticola*, **a.** enlarged, **b.** larva

183. Blackbird taking earthworm **184.** Starling taking insect **185.** Frit fly, *Oscinis frit*, **a.** fly, larva and pupa, enlarged **186.** Crane fly, *Tipula paludosa*, **a.** larva and pupa, enlarged **187.** Seagull taking Chafer larva

183

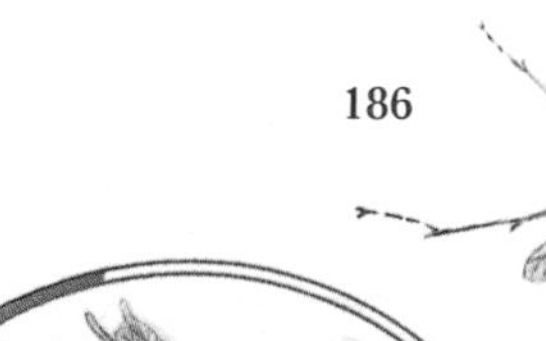

186

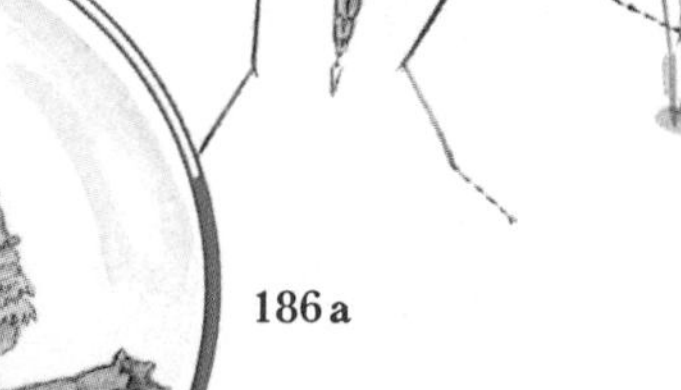

186 a

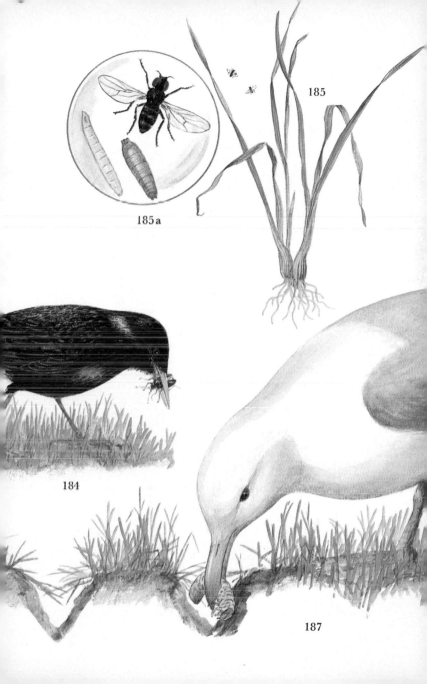

185

185 a

184

187

188

188a

188. Fairy rings caused by fungi, **a.** fruiting bodies, enlarged **189.** Greying of grass by *Fusarium nivale* **190.** Dollar spot, *Sclerotinia homoeocarpa* **191.** Fungus disease, *Diachaea leucopoda*, **a.** enlarged

189

190

191

191 a

192

193

192. Damage after uneven application of fertiliser **193.** Ants, *Formicidae*, on concrete path **194.** Scorching caused by dog urine **195.** Scorching caused by the fungus *Corticium fuciforme*, **a.** enlarged **196.** Click beetle, *Agriotes obscurus*, **a.** beetle and larva enlarged

194

195

195a

196

196a

Tulips

197   198

199   200

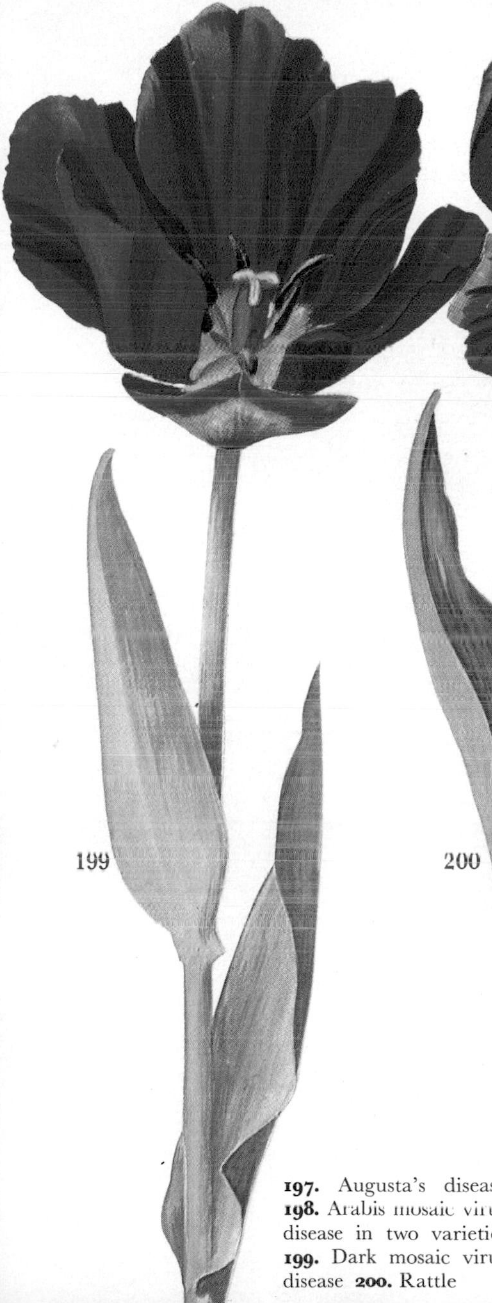

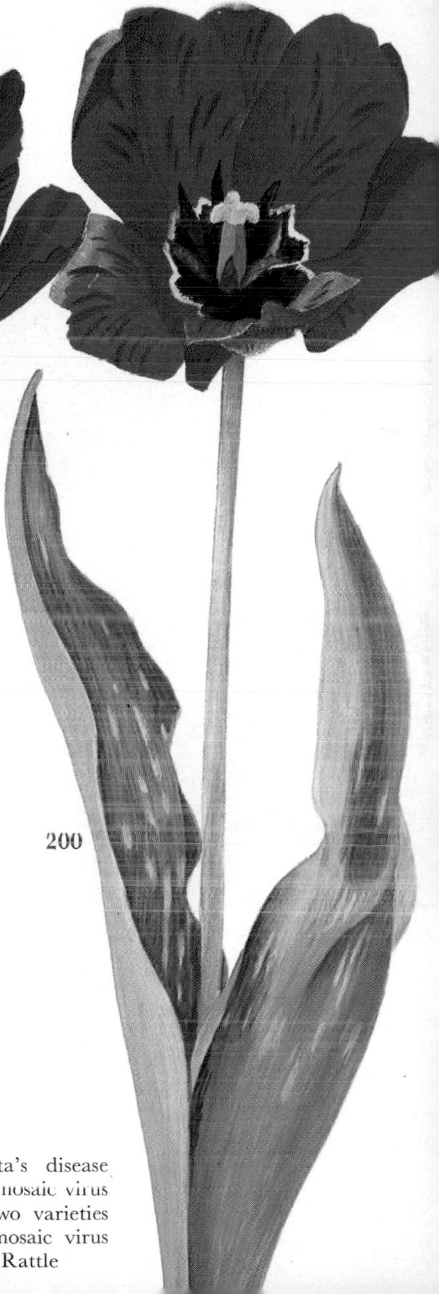

197. Augusta's disease
198. Arabis mosaic virus
disease in two varieties
199. Dark mosaic virus
disease **200.** Rattle

201. Three healthy flowers of the same variety 'Gudoshnik'. **202.** Heat damage, **a.** medium, **b.** severe, **c.** killed **203.** Cucumber mosaic virus disease

201

202

202 a

203

202 b

202 c

204. Tulip fire, *Botrytis tulipae*, **a.** spore bodies on bulb
205–206. Tulip 'sports', **a.** original varieties **207.** Grey bulb rot, *Sclerotium tuliparum*, **a.** longitudinal section of bulb

204

205 a

204 a

205   206 a   206

207   207 a

208. Mosaic virus disease **209.** Chocolate spot **210.** Silver leaf **211.** Blind buds

210

211

212c

213

212

212b

212a

213 a

212. Narcissus fire, *Botrytis narcissicola*, **a.** longitudinal section of bulb, **b.** enlarged, **c.** spore bodies on bulb **213.** Attack of Tarsonemid bulb mite, *Rhizoglyphus echinopus*, **a.** enlarged **214.** Bulb rot, *Fusarium oxysporum*, in longitudinal section of bulb **215.** Grassiness (physiological)

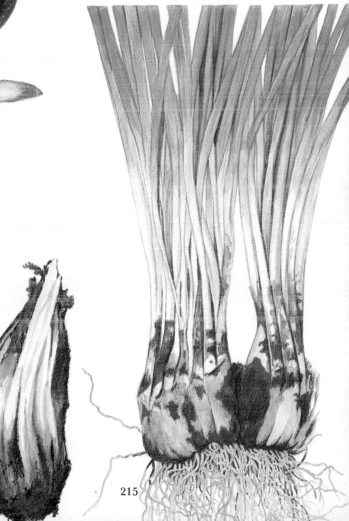

214 215

216

216a

217

218

219   220   220a   221

216. Stem eelworm, *Ditylenchus dipsaci*, **a.** cross section of bulb **217.** Larva of the Large Narcissus fly, *Merodon equestris* **218.** Larvae of the Small Narcissus fly, *Eumerus tuberculatus* **219.** Heat damage on leaves **220.** Heat damage on blooms, **a.** healthy bloom **221.** Cold damage

222. Sparrow pecking Crocus blooms **223.** Rattle **224.** Mosaic virus disease, **a.** healthy plant **225.** Bloom stripe caused by virus disease **226.** Zig-zag leaf, physiological disorder

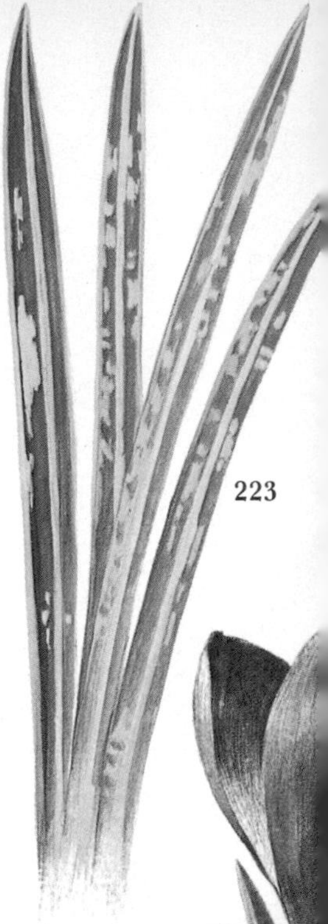

223

222

226

224 a 224 225

227. Rattle **228.** Soft rot, *Xanthomonas hyacinthi*, cross and longitudinal sections of bulb **229.** Mosaic virus disease, severe and mild attack, **a.** healthy flower spike **230.** Loose bud

227

228

229

229 a

230

Dahlia

231. Attack by green capsid, *Lygus pabulinus*, **a.** capsid, enlarged **232.** Earwig, *Forficula auricularia*, **a.** enlarged **233.** Dahlia smut, *Entyloma dahliae* **234.** Mosaic virus disease, **a.** healthy bloom **235.** Cabbage moth, *Barathra brassicae*, **a.** larva, **b.** pupa

233

234

234 a

235 a

235

235 b

236 a

236

236. Mosaic virus disease in leaf and flowers, **a.** healthy flower **237.** Gladiolus thrips, *Taeniothrips simplex*, on leaves and single flower **238.** Leaf spot disease, *Septoria gladioli*, **a.** enlarged **239.** Hard rot, *Septoria gladioli*, in corm

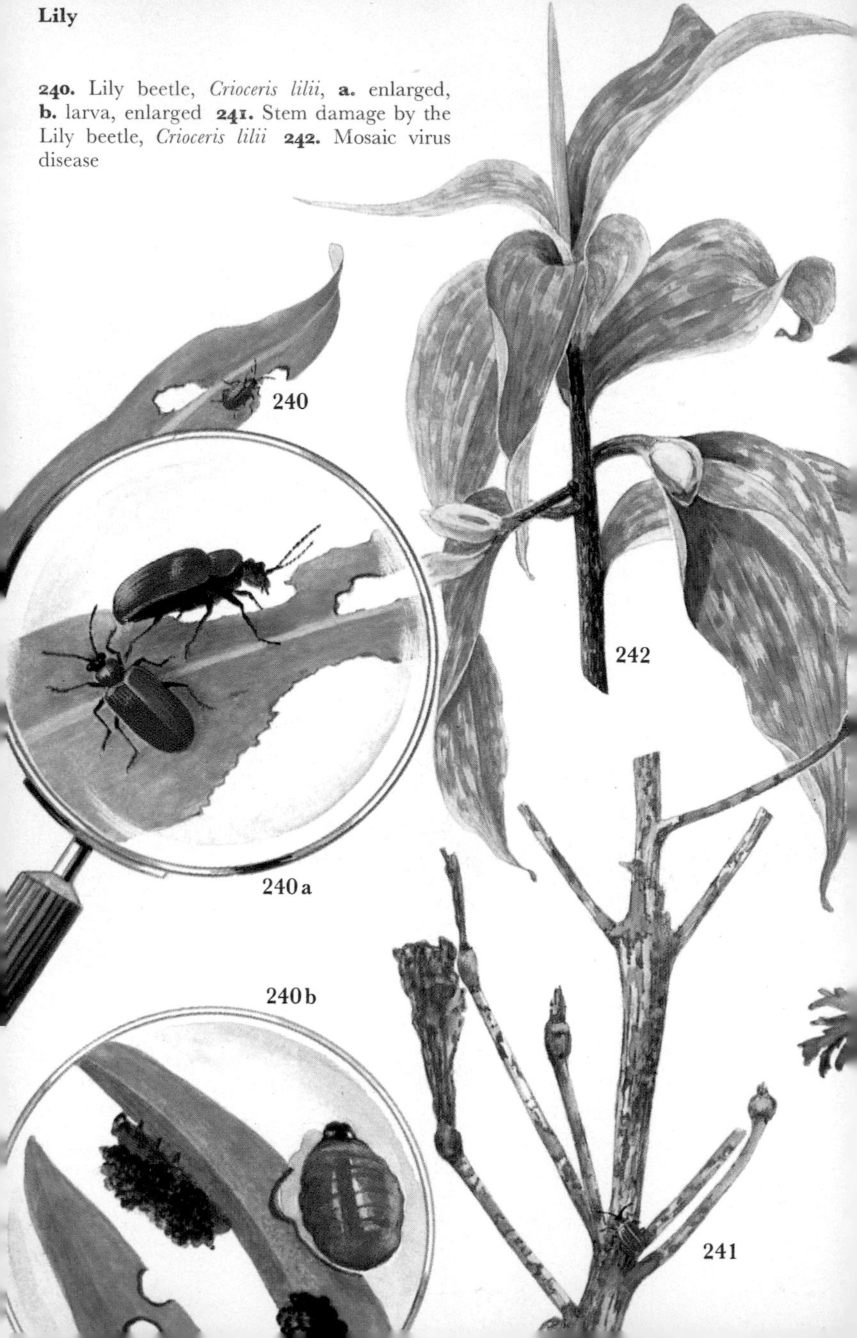

Lily

240. Lily beetle, *Crioceris lilii*, **a.** enlarged,
b. larva, enlarged **241.** Stem damage by the
Lily beetle, *Crioceris lilii* **242.** Mosaic virus
disease

240

240 a

240 b

242

241

243. Anemone rust, *Tranz-schelia pruni-spinosae*, on De Caen, *Anemone coronaria* 244. Blind bud in De Caen, *Anemone coronaria*, **a.** healthy flower 245. Cold damage

246. Attack of Leaf miner, *Phytomyza minuscula*, on Aquilegia **247.** Hollyhock rust, *Puccinia malvacearum*, **a.** enlarged

248. Paeony grey mould, *Botrytis paeoniae*, **a.** enlarged **249.** Mosaic virus disease in Delphinium

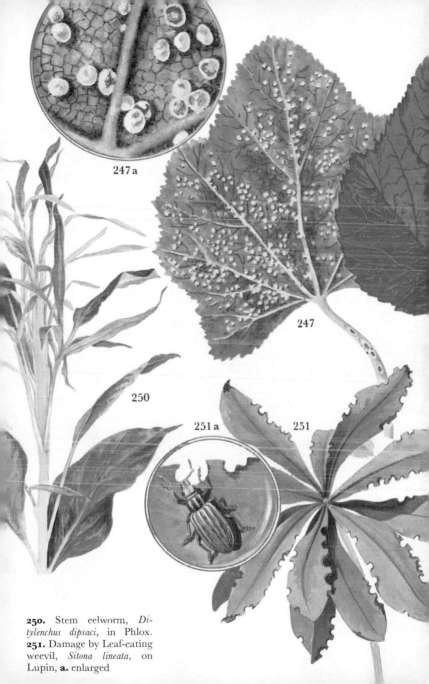

250. Stem eelworm, *Ditylenchus dipsaci*, in Phlox.
251. Damage by Leaf-eating
weevil, *Sitona lineata*, on
Lupin, **a.** enlarged

252

253

254 a

254

255

252. Leaf spot disease, *Septoria phlogis*, on Phlox **253.** Leaf spot disease, *Phyllosticta trollii*, on Globe Flower (*Trollius*), **a.** lower surface of leaf **254.** Anemone fire, *Tuburcina anemones*, on Globe Flower (*Trollius*), **a.** healthy flower **255.** Christmas Rose mildew, *Peronospora pulveracea*, on Christmas Rose (*Helleborus niger*), **a.** detail **256.** Leaf spot, *Coniothyrium hellebori*

257

258

257. Attack of Leaf miner, *Chylizosoma vittatum*, on Solomon's Seal (*Polygonatum*) **258.** Damage by larvae of Leaf sawfly, *Phymatocera aterrima*, on Solomon's Seal (*Polygonatum*) **259.** Silver Y moth, *Plusia gamma*, **a.** larva **260.** Mosaic virus disease in Bleeding Heart (*Dicentra*).

259

259 a

260

261 a   261

265

266

265 b   265 a

261. Cuckoo spit of Leaf frog hopper, *Philaenus spumarius*, **a.** Frog hopper enlarged **262.** Leaf aphid, *Aphis sp.*, on Marsh Marigold (*Caltha*) **263.** Grey mould, *Botrytis cinerea*, on Chrysanthemum **264.** Leaf miner tunnels of *Phytomyza atricornis* in Chrysanthemum leaf **265.** Turnip moth, *Agrotis segetum*, on Primula, **a.** caterpillar (cutworm), **b.** pupa **266.** Grey field slug, *Agriolimax reticulatus*, and damage on Lily-of-the-Valley (*Convallaria*) **267.** Wood snail, *Cepaea nemoralis*, and damage on Lily-of-the-Valley (*Convallaria*)

268

269 a

269

270 a

270

268. Mosaic virus disease of Sweet Pea (*Lathyrus*)
269. Thrips, *Thrips spp.*, on Asters, **a.** larva and adult, enlarged **270.** Flea beetle, *Phyllotreta spp.*, on Alyssum, **a.** enlarged **271.** Thrips, *Thrips spp.*, on Marigold (*Calendula*) **272.** Powdery mildew, *Erysiphe cichoracearum*, on Marigold (*Calendula*) **273.** Cabbage White butterflies, *Pieris brassicae*, on Wallflower (*Cheiranthus*) **a.** caterpillar

271

272

273 a

273

274. Sclerotinia disease, *Sclerotinia sclerotiorum*, on Sunflower (*Helianthus*), **a.** cut stem, enlarged **275.** Root rot disease, *Pythium spp.*, in Zinnia **276.** Mosaic virus disease of Geranium **277.** Pelargonium rust, *Puccinia pelargonii zonalis*, **a.** upper leaf surface **278.** Crown gall bacterial disease, *Corynebacterium fascians*

274

275

274 a

Pelargonium

276

277   277 a

278

279

279. Iron deficiency
280. Manganese deficiency
281. Potash deficiency
282-284. Magnesium deficiency

280

281

282

283

284

285. Damage by wood preservatives on Privet (*Ligustrum*) **286.** Damage by wood preservatives on Tulip flower **287.** Hail damage on Lupin **288.** Hail damage on short-stemmed leaf of deciduous tree **289.** Damage by weedkiller on Plane tree (*Platanus*), **a.** healthy leaf **290.** Damage by weedkiller on Rose **291.** Damage by weedkiller on Maple (*Acer*), **a.** healthy leaf

289 a

289

290

291

291 a

292. Short-tailed field mouse (Vole)
293. Red mouse
294. Mole, **a.** mole mound
295. Water rat

292

294 a

294

293

295

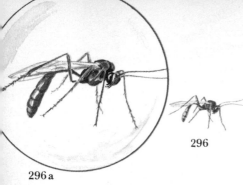

296 a

296

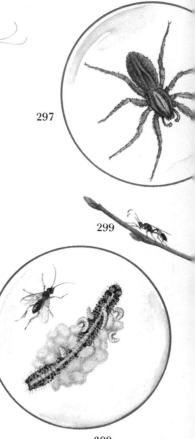

297

299

300

296. Ichneumon or Sail wasp, *Ophion sp.*, **a.** enlarged **297.** Hunting spider, *Tarentula pulverulenta*, enlarged **298.** Garden spider, *Meta segmentata* **299.** Parasitic wasp, *Ichneumon sp.* **300.** Parasitic wasp, *Apantales glomeratus*, and larvae with and without cocoon on cabbage caterpillar, enlarged **301.** Rove beetle, *Staphylinus olens* **302.** Carabid beetle, *Carabus violaceus*, enlarged, **a.** larva **303.** Centipede, *Pachymerium ferrugineum* **304.** Predaceous capsid, *Anthocoris nemorum*, enlarged **305.** Aphid consumed by the larva of the parasitic wasp, *Aphidius sp.*

301

302

302 a

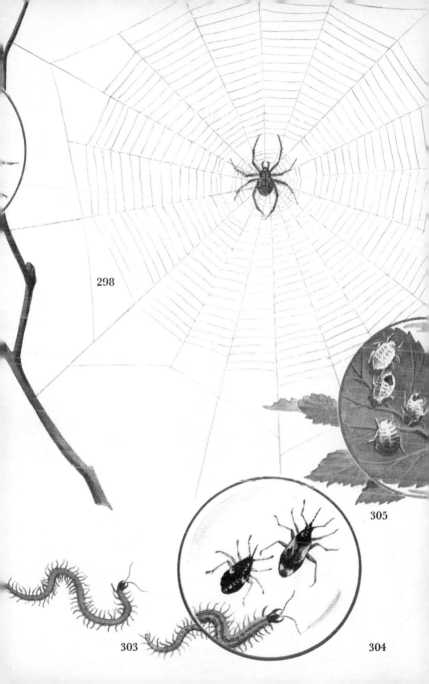

298

305

303

304

306

306a

310b

310

310a

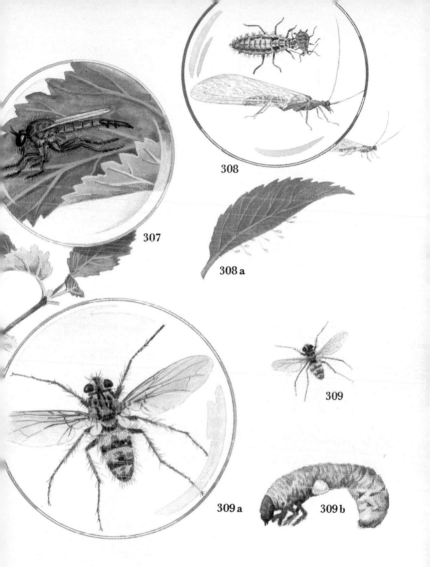

306. Hover fly, *Syrphus balteatus*, **a.** fly, larva and pupa enlarged **307.** Robber fly, *Neoitamus cyanurus*, enlarged **308.** Lacewing, *Chrysopa carnea*, with larva, enlarged **309.** Parasitic fly, *Dexiosoma caninum*, **a.** enlarged, **b.** larva, boring slowly into a chafer grub **310.** Ladybird, *Coccinella septempunctata*, and larva, **a.** enlarged, **b.** pupa, enlarged

311. Titmouse, **a.** blue tit
312. Hedgehog
313. Common toad

PESTS AND DISEASES

The following notes are supplementary to those with the colour illustrations and are in the same numerical order. They explain the respective cause of plant damage, the development and degree of damage caused, and control measures. The latter is dealt with in more detail under Control Measures and Methods, p. 15. It will be noted that the types of damage are listed under plant species, e.g. Fir (*Abies*), Spruce (*Picea*), Pine (*Pinus*), Larch (*Larix*), Conifers, etc., since different symptoms are sometimes produced by the same pest or disease on different plants. Where this is the case, reference is made under the appropriate heading.

1 Fir Rust, *Pucciniastrum pustulatum*
The infected needles turn yellow-green in June and wilt away completely later. Small, yellow-white, tube-shaped growths can be seen on the lower surfaces of the needles from which will emerge the red-yellow spores. There are several types of rust of fir trees which have various weeds as the alternate hosts, the most important of these being willow herb. The fir tree may be weakened by a severe attack, but this normally only occurs if there is a large amount of willow herb near the tree. Treatment is difficult and only in the case of small, valuable plants should thorough spraying be carried out in the spring and early summer using one of the products controlling rust fungi.

2 Damage by night frost
In the first few weeks after the buds have emerged and while they are still soft, there is a danger of them being killed by frost. If this occurs, normal end buds will in most cases not develop until the following spring.

By placing cut branches from other conifers around and in between the new plantings some of the damage can be prevented. This method is not practicable if the trees are more than five years old.

3 Transplanting damage on Noble Fir, *Abies nobilis*
The needles turn brown to red-brown but do not drop off. The buds on the end of the branches do not develop or produce new shoots. This particular type of plant often reacts very strongly to the change in soil and climatic conditions which can occur during transplanting. The trees may stagnate for two or three years before shooting again and then continue to grow normally. There is no preventive measure or treatment, just patience while the tree re-adapts itself.

4 Silver Fir Adelges, *Dreyfusia nordmannianae*
This species lives in colonies and in the summer it can be found crowded on the new shoots, each aphid

(adelges) being about 0·5 mm long. Both the needles and shoots acquire a yellowish discolouration and become curled and bent, and there may be some wilting at the top of the tree. Some of the aphids develop wings and fly off to new hosts, but most remain wingless. After the winter, the wax-covered females emerge and lay their eggs on the shoots. These eggs usually hatch during May and June at the same time as the new shoots are beginning to grow. The Silver Fir adelges is really a host-changing species but since its main host, the Oriental Spruce (*Picea orientalis*), is rarely grown in the U.K. it has to live most of its life cycle on the *Abies* varieties, of which the Caucasian Fir (*Abies nordmanniana*) and the Silver Fir (*Abies alba*) are the favourites. The attack can be treated by heavy watering over the trees if they are not too large, or they can be sprayed with an insecticide either in the early spring or late September.

5 Green Pineapple Gall Aphid, *Sacciphantes viridis*

Pineapple or stawberry galls and other similar deformities are formed by the so-called *Chermes* species. The green pineapple gall aphid is the most common on Norway Spruce (*Picea abies*). Both species form the 2–3 cm-long galls on the shoots. If one of the galls is opened, masses of the aphids can be found in the many small chambers. The green pineapple gall aphid is a good example of a host-changing species. It overwinters under the bark scales of the European Larch (*Larix decidua*) and during the spring a winged generation develops. These fly to the Norway Spruce or other *Picea* species where the offspring of the winged forms make the galls and from these a return to the larch takes place in the autumn. If the weather is favourable the multiplication could be almost explosive (see Black Aphid, no. 262). It may therefore be necessary to protect the younger spruce trees against severe attack with insecticides, and these can produce good results when the aphids are not protected by the galls. Spraying should therefore be done in April or September. If the attack is not severe it can be controlled by picking off the galls.

6 Winter or frost damage

This is recognisable by yellow to brown needles and possibly dead end buds in spring and summer. The cause is a combination of severe frost interrupted by periods of mild weather with the temperature well above freezing. The large variations in temperature cause the plant tissue to be held back in one period and stimulated to growth in the next. The sharper the temperature changes, the more severe the damage to the plants. Pruning of wilted parts of the plants should not be carried out until the late spring at the earliest.

7 Douglas Fir Aphid, *Gilletteella cooleyi*

On Sitka Spruce (*Picea sitchensis*) and White Spruce (*Picea glauca*) an attack by this aphid will produce red-violet galls of up to 6 cm in length. The white, wax-covered aphids often form large colonies on Douglas Fir (*Pseudotsuga taxifolia*). The life cycle resembles that of the Silver Fir adelges (no. 4). A host change takes place between Douglas Fir and Sitka Spruce as well as certain other *Picea* species. The attack is not significant under good growing conditions.

8 Strawberry Gall Aphid, *Adelges tardus*

This aphid may form the characteristic galls on various *Picea* species but the damage is not significant where the trees are growing under good conditions.

9 Sitka Spruce Aphid, *Neomyzaphis abietina*

Considerable damage can be caused to several *Picea* species by this aphid, particularly Sitka Spruce (*Picea sitchensis*) and White Spruce (*Picea glauca*) which can suffer from loss of needles. The Sitka Spruce aphid can thrive in quite low temperatures and reproduction commences early in spring, reaching its peak in May–June. The attack can be very damaging after a mild winter, and it may then be necessary to protect the younger spruce trees with an insecticide spray during May.

10 Vapourer Moth Caterpillar, *Orgyia antiqua*

During a severe attack by this interesting, web-spinning caterpillar, both conifers and deciduous trees and bushes can be completely stripped. Only the male moth can fly, the female only has rudimentary wings. The female stays all the time near the web where she has emerged from the pupa. She also lays the greyish egg masses here. The newly hatched larvae spin a short thread and, like young spiders, can be carried long distances by the wind. The damage by the caterpillars is seen mostly in June–July. When they are fully grown, about 3 cm long, they crawl onto stone walls and planks where they spin their cocoons. There may be years between bad attacks, since natural enemies will often clear up a quite severe outbreak. As long as the caterpillars are small, under 1 cm long, they can be controlled with insecticides, but the older, longer larvae are much more difficult to control with chemicals.

11 Cucurbitaria piceae

This fungus disease causes the end buds on the tip of the shoots to stop growing and developing, so that the new growth of the trees is very restricted. On close examination a large number of black, ball-shaped growths can be seen crowded on the bud. The disease is uncommon, and the only remedy is to cut off any branches damaged by it.

12 Spruce Needle Roller, *Eucosma tedella*

This small greyish moth has caterpillars, barely 1 cm long, which spoil the branches of the Spruce by spinning together and eating into the needles which become brown and enclosed in a web containing granular excreta. The symptoms of an attack do not show up clearly until late summer or early autumn, but a careful watch should be kept from early August for the small larvae. If they are present in considerable numbers spraying with a suitable insecticide will easily control them.

13 Conifer Spider Mite,
Oligonychus ununguis

A small red-yellow spider mite which is found mainly on firs, spruces and junipers. The web production is only small, but the feeding by the mites causes the needles to become a spotted green-yellow. In a severe attack the needles on the affected shoots turn completely brown. This species overwinters as the egg. During the summer there are four to five generations, the eggs of which are yellow and can be found in the young shoots. Their control is principally by providing the plant with good growing conditions so that damage is minimised. Chemical treatment is difficult but can possibly be tried during warm weather in the middle of summer.

14 Nun Moth, *Lymantria monacha*

In the years when there is an outbreak of the caterpillars of this moth much damage can be done to conifers, but deciduous trees are rarely attacked. Firs and spruces, in particular, can be so severely stripped in early summer that they die. The fully grown caterpillars turn into the chrysalis stage on the branches where later in the summer they hatch into the pretty white moth. The eggs are laid on the bark and overwinter, the young larvae emerging in the spring. Control is not easy, although some insecticides are effective just after the eggs have hatched.

15 Large Bark Beetle,
Dendroctonus micans

A brownish black beetle, nearly 1 cm long, which lays its eggs in the early summer in masses of over a hundred in small chambers in the bark. The larvae widen these chambers which then get filled with a mixture of excreta and resin. This mixture often extrudes from the stem and drops down in irregular brownish lumps. In addition to Norway Spruce (*Picea abies*), Blue Spruce (*Picea pungens*), White Spruce (*Picea glauca*) and Sitka Spruce (*Picea sitchensis*) are attacked, but it is only the larger trees and these can live for many years with the damage, provided they can have good growing conditions. Control is possible with lindane.

16 Typograph Bark Beetle, *Ips typographus*

This beetle, which is about half a centimetre long, bores passages into the inner layer of bark and the outer layer of wood and is thus a typical bark beetle. Most of the bark beetles have their characteristic passage systems and the Typograph beetle can easily be identified by the 10–15 cm-long mother passages where the eggs are laid. Branching off from this main passage are masses of shorter passages, formed as the larvae feed their way through. As the Typograph beetle prefers to breed in weakened spruce trees, especially Norway Spruce (*Picea abies*), it is important to keep the trees healthy by giving them plenty of space in which to grow. Fallen trees should be removed as they often serve as breeding sites. This beetle rarely breeds in the U.K., but is sometimes imported in timber. Chemical treatment of trees to control it is useless.

17 Root Disease or White Pocket Rot, *Fomes annosus*

The symptoms of the disease above ground are that the needles first become dull and then greyish. Later they become yellow, wilt, turn brown and drop off. The fungus grows from the soil into the roots and then further up the stem. The tree steadily deteriorates and finally dies. White fruiting bodies from the fungus may develop on the surface of the soil but are often overlooked. Fencing poles are often a source of infection and it is important that these are thoroughly impregnated with creosote before use. When trees are cut down the stumps should either be dug up or treated with a recommended chemical, or with the latest method of biological control which consists of using *Peniophora gigantea*, a competing but harmless fungus. If the disease has been confirmed in a tree then it should be cut down and destroyed with its main roots. In the following years it is preferable to only plant herbaceous plants in the infected plot. Root disease can attack a large number of conifer species but Silver Fir (*Abies*) is resistant. Deciduous trees, with the exception of Thorns (*Crataegus*), are resistant.

18 Stem strangulation by Honeysuckle, *Lonicera periclymenum*

The honeysuckle can sometimes wind itself so tightly around the stem of young trees that strangulation marks appear, and there is an effect on the stem growth and overall vigour of the tree.

19 Pine Bark Blister Rust, *Cronartium ribicola*

In May a considerable number of white-yellow blisters, half a centimetre in diameter, develop on the bark of older branches. The diseased part of the branch is swollen for a length of 20–40 cm. Later the blisters burst open and a cloud of red-brown spore dust comes out. The attacked branches wilt and die. The disease actually consists of two types, one of which has a host change with certain weeds, and the other is transmitted direct from conifer to conifer. It is impossible for a lay person to distinguish between the two. Infected branches must be cut out and destroyed before the disease can infect other conifers.

20 Needleless part of branch after male flower

A short distance from the end bud on a shoot the branch will often be without needles, as if it had been attacked by a fungus disease or pests. This, however, is quite normal. The production of male flowers in the early summer was so plentiful that the tree was unable to produce needles on this part of the branch at the same time. Needles will not be produced at all on this particular part of the branch.

21 Pine Bark Blister Rust, *Cronartium pini*

The symptoms are very similar to those of no. 19, the difference being that in this case it is the five-needled pine which is attacked, primarily Weymouth Pine (*Pinus strobus*). The disease has an alternate host in the Blackcurrant (*Ribes nigrum*) and other

Ribes species, whose leaf under-surfaces become covered with a red-brown felt-like layer, called Black-currant Felt Rust, late in the summer. If the pine trees are considered the most valuable ones in the garden then it is preferable not to cultivate any *Ribes* bushes.

22 Pine Needle Blister Rust,
Coleosporium pini

In May–June yellow to yellow-brown small blisters may develop on the needles of the double-needled pines. These blisters are only about 2 mm across, but they cause the needles to wilt and often to die. There are alternate hosts, Groundsel (*Senecio vulgaris*) being the most common. The damage is normally very slight and the attack not widespread.

23 Drying-out Disease of buds and branches, *Scleroderris lagerbergii*

This fungus disease causes the needles around the end buds to become brown during the winter, and the bud does not develop into a shoot in the summer but stays in its bud sheaths. The damage may occur on a large number of branches, but always on the end shoots. The disease is worst when the latter part of the summer has been cold and wet and the trees are rather over-crowded. The degree of damage varies considerably from year to year and the only control possible is to remove branches which have the disease.

24 Winter damage

In northern areas winter damage can appear as yellow, yellow-brown or completely brown needles on one-and two-year-old branches. Normally the end buds are not destroyed, and therefore the new growth will not be affected. In exposed areas a strong wind will dry out the needles and increase the winter damage. If pine trees suffering from winter damage are in a prominent position in the garden they should be pruned.

25 Hare damage

During the winter young trees of different species can be damaged by the feeding of hares. The damage on conifers is primarily of an aesthetic nature as the trees rarely suffer any further damage. To protect plants, a fence can be erected or each tree surrounded with chicken wire. There are also repellent preparations for smearing on the stem and branches.

26 Pine Needle-Sheath Gall Midge, *Thecodiplosis brachyntera*

After a night frost in the autumn, groups of needles on the Mountain Pine (*Pinus mugo*) or Forest Pine (*Pinus sylvestris*) will sometimes change colour from green to yellow. A careful inspection among the needles will reveal a small gall with a 2–3 mm-long red larva inside. The attacked needles, in addition to being dis-coloured, may also be shorter and distorted. The gall midge usually flies during May and on sunny, warm days it is possible to watch the red female laying her eggs on top of the shoot point. Mild attacks do not cause any damage, but a severe attack can spoil young trees and also provide an entry for fungus diseases. Healthy, strong growing trees will withstand any attack much better and it is essential to provide new plantings with plenty of water. The yellow needles should be removed in the autumn and burned, while insecticides can be effective during the midge's flying period.

27 Pine Sawfly, *Lophyrus pini*

Colonies of sawfly caterpillars on a two-year-old branch can completely strip it of needles. The larvae are green and up to 3 cm long. An attack can take place both in May–June and again in July–September. In a heavy infestation of these caterpillars a virus disease is sometimes present. A sign of this is that many caterpillars will hang limply from the needles and branches. If the dead larvae are collected and put in a bucket of water, the water, after a couple of days, will contain virus particles and can be effectively sprayed onto healthy colonies of caterpillars. In addition to this biological method of control, insecticides can be successfully used when the larvae are small.

28 Pine Sawfly, *Lophyrus pini*

The adult sawflys can often be seen in spring as they fly among the pine tree branches, laying their eggs in rows on the newly developing needles. Details of the larvae are given in no. 27. A second generation is produced later in the summer. Several other sawflies may attack pine trees in a similar manner.

29 Woodpecker damage

This can often be seen in gardens on the older trees after the various species of woodpeckers have been pecking at the bark in their search for insects. They often place the cones in the fork of a branch so that they can split them more easily in order to reach the seeds. Underneath and around such a woodpecker's 'workshop' there is usually a large number of damaged cones.

30 Pine Shoot Moth, *Evetria buoliana*

This is a small reddish moth which flies and lays its eggs about midsummer. The larvae emerge in the autumn and feed on needles and buds. They overwinter in hollowed buds and move to healthy buds at the end of March to early April. The new buds are eaten in such a manner that the growing point becomes distorted or completely inverts. In gardens it is usually sufficient to gather and burn the attacked shoots with their red-brown caterpillars. In cases of larger outbreaks, insecticides can be used in the spring at the time the caterpillars are moving from hibernation.

31 Pine Stem Aphid, *Pineus pini*

This aphid can sometimes form colonies on the stem and branches of the Mountain Pine (*Pinus mugo*) and Forest Pine (*Pinus sylvestris*), preferring trees which are growing either under dry or very wet conditions. In the first case suitable watering with liberal sprinkling can help the plants over the attack, while in the latter case drainage is required.

32 Needle Drop Disease, *Meria laricis*

On trees up to five years old, the oldest needles may turn yellow and drop off. Since the disease only overwinters in the infected needles, these should be collected and burnt.

33 Larch Canker, *Dasyscypha willkommii*

The symptoms of larch canker are a massive drop of needles or a lack of needle development in the spring associated with swellings and more or less open wounds on older branches, and these can appear on older trees which had previously been growing quite satisfactorily. If the disease can be diagnosed at an early stage the wounds should be thoroughly treated with a canker and wound healing compound, and if necessary the treatment repeated after a few weeks. If, however, the disease has reached an advanced stage the only treatment is to cut off and burn all the infected branches.

34 Green Pineapple Gall Aphid, *Sacchiphantes viridis*

This aphid can occur partly on European Larch (*Larix decidua*) and partly on Norway Spruce (*Picea abies*), (see no. 5).

35 Roe deer horn rubbing

This can be especially annoying on young trees planted in parks or country gardens. The bark is destroyed and the trees must recommence to form new shoots under the damaged stem. The deer may also bite off the main shoot. The erection of a deer fence may be necessary, although the damage can often be prevented by the use of one of the animal repellent products now available.

36 Larch Needle Miner, *Coleophora laricinella*

If the outer parts of the needles become white it is usually caused by the presence of the tiny larvae of this moth inside them. The larvae, only a few millimetres long, bite off the needle tips in the autumn and overwinter at the base of the shoot, or under the bark. In the spring they emerge and feed on needles and buds until they pupate. Light attacks do not cause any significant damage, but if large numbers are present an insecticide spray is justified.

37 Larch Cone Moth, *Dioryctria abietella*

The larvae of this insignificant little night-flying moth are reddish and up to 2 cm long and will eat through the cones of various conifers. Even more damaging is the attack on top shoots which are hollowed out and filled with granular excreta. The attacked cones and shoots should be cut off and burned with the larvae inside.

38 Spruce Spinning Mite, *Oligonychus ununguis*

During the summer the tiny, red-yellow spinning mites swarm in between the needles which turn a spotted greenish-yellow. (For further details see no. 13.)

39 Juniper Moth, *Nothris marginella*

The caterpillars are grey with a red stripe down each side. They feed on and weave together the needles of the juniper bushes, giving the bushes a scruffy appearance. The plain, grey moth flys during the middle of summer. Treatment with insecticides can take place if necessary during July.

40 Winter damage

The symptoms of damage vary according to variety and species, from yellow to brown and red-violet discolouring of the needles. If the damage is severe, the buds will also be destroyed and then pruning must be done. (See also no. 42.)

41 Juniper Tongue Rust,
Gymnosporangium clavariaeforme
This disease is often seen on the pillar-shaped varieties where the branches will swell for a length of 5–10 cm. At the attacked places red-brown tongues, about half a centimetre long, develop in May. These may, in damp weather, become 1–1½ cm long and a more yellow colour. Although the disease rarely destroys the bush, badly infected branches will wilt and die in the course of a few years. The disease has an alternate host in the Hawthorn (*Crataegus*), but the symptoms are completely different. (See no. 70.)

42 Branch Death, *Phomopsis juniperovora* or *Kabatina juniperi*
Branch death can be caused by one of two fungi. It becomes apparent in the early summer with brown or black-brown needles, on wilted parts on the branches, which often resemble winter damage (no. 40). The two fungi cannot be distinguished with the naked eye. In addition to pruning the damaged branches, the affected bushes can be sprayed during the summer with a suitable fungicide.

43 Juniper Gall Rust,
Gymnosporangium sabinae
The fungus develops on the older branches where large swellings can be observed. In April–May these are covered in a jelly-like brown-grey substance. All junipers, and in particular Savin (*Juniperus sabina*), weaken and fade away when severely attacked, but this may take up to ten years. The fungus has an alternate host in the Pear (*Pyrus*) where it forms red spots on the leaves. These are fairly few and it does no harm to the tree. There is no method of control.

44 Leaf Aphid, *Lachniella sp.*
Quite large aphids make their appearance at times on the older branches of *Thuja* and are called branch aphids. The black sooty mould thrives on the sugary honeydew excreted by these aphids. If the attack is heavy the plants must be sprayed with an insecticide. A jet of water can be used to wash off the insects if they are not too numerous.

45 Thuja Scale, *Eulecanium arion*
These small, scale-covered insects suck the plant juices with a specially adapted tube-shaped mouth, like the aphids. On some evergreen plants the damage can be quite considerable. As long as they remain under their scale, these aphid-like insects are well protected against insecticides, and unless systemic insecticides are used, the only method of controlling them chemically is in the 'free phase'. During the summer the larvae emerge from under the mother scale and move to a new area to make their own scale. With the help of a magnifying glass it is possible to observe the development of the larvae and when several of them appear on the branches spraying should begin.

46 Abnormal growth caused by poor soil conditions

Hedge plants, and sometimes individual trees, may be spoiled by a slight abnormal annual growth or unsatisfactory colour. The cause can be aphids (no. 44), but deformed growth on top can be directly associated with unsatisfactory root functioning. The illustration shows strong, well-functioning roots in the upper layer of soil, while there are only a few poorly developed roots further down, which can only absorb water and salts to a very limited degree. It is apparent that the soil is very poor, both physically and chemically, and also lacks air due to poor drainage. Hot spells in the summer increase the demand on the functioning of the roots and these, associated with dry periods when the plants can only obtain water and nutrients from the upper layers of the soil, result in malnutrition. If this type of abnormal growth has been ascertained, the soil around the plants should be improved by digging and fertilising both in the spring and autumn.

47 Thuja Leaf Spot Disease, *Didymascella thujina*

In hedges, but also sometimes in individual *Thuja*, a number of adjacent branches become yellow-green and red-brown in colour. After some time the plant appears to open out as the wilted branches drop off. If the yellow and yellow-brown shoot tips are examined under a magnifying glass, a small brown-black growth, 0·5–1 mm in size, can be seen on the occasional needle. Late in the summer the needle falls off and leaves

a small hole. When the humidity is high, as is often the case in an enclosed garden, the disease will spread rapidly. Spraying with a fungicide late in the summer will control it.

48 Bark Weevil, *Otiorrhynchus sulcatus*

This black weevil, 1 cm long, eats the bark and needles on young shoots. The white larvae, which have a brown head, feed on the roots. Biological control is discussed, no. 148.

49 Yew Scale, *Eulecanium crudum*

This insect forms a red-brown, oval scale, about 3 mm long, on the older shoots. The yellow larvae are mostly found on the needles and young shoots. The black sooty mould fungus grows freely in the honey-dew excreted by these insects. The larvae can be killed with insecticide in July.

50 Frost damage

The needles of the Yew (*Taxus*) become yellow and drained of colour when damaged by frost. Only very rarely do all the needles on a shoot become brown. It closely resembles frost damage on *Picea* (no. 6).

51 Gall Mite, *Eriophyes psilaspis*

This microscopic, oblong mite lives inside thickened leaves and buds, which, because of the attack, do not unfold in the spring. In the summer the plant produces new buds, but these are also attacked and eventually destroyed. The shoots may develop after a light attack, but they will be shorter and have deformed needles. A sulphur spray applied a few times during August and September can be effective.

52 **Box Gall Midge,**
Monarthropalpus buxi

The Box gall midge is about 2 mm long and flies around during May and June laying eggs inside the leaves and tips of shoots. Later in the summer yellowish spots can be seen on the upper surface of leaves, and bubble-shaped mines on the lower surface. If a mine is opened the orange-coloured larva can be found inside. The larvae overwinter in the mines and pupation takes place in May. Just before emerging as an adult the pupa works itself half-way out through a hole in the lower surface of the leaf, and when the midge emerges it leaves the empty pupa skin behind in the leaf. The attacked shoots can be cut off and destroyed during the winter and this reduces the infestation. Insecticides can be used if the attack is heavy enough to justify it.

53 **Box Leaf Sucker,** *Psylla buxi*

The adult leaf sucker is approximately 4 mm long, with glass-clear wings. It appears on the plants in July and August and lays its eggs on the outer scale of the buds at the tips of the branches. The larvae overwinter where they emerge and in the spring suck the young leaves causing them to become spoon-shaped and curled upwards. The sooty mould fungus often grows on the excreta from the larvae. Insecticide treatment in July is effective against the adult leaf sucker.

54 **Mahonia Rust,** *Cunminsiella sanguinea*

This fungus disease produces yellow to red or red-violet spots of varying intensity. On the lower surface of the leaves, a few small, brown, raised spots will form. The red colour can be very attractive and is sometimes used decoratively in flower and plant arrangements. If dark green leaves are preferred, an appropriate fungicide should be used in the spring

55 **Winter damage of Mahonia**

This is recognised by grey-brown to brown discolourations indicating those parts of the plant which have been killed. The discolouration appears in the spring and usually only on the leaves produced the previous summer since older leaves are able to withstand the winter better. As previously mentioned (no. 6), wide fluctuations in temperature are often the main cause of this damage. If the roots are frozen, the leaves may wilt and dry out completely since water evaporating from the leaves cannot be replaced by water absorbed through the roots. Protection during the winter with cut spruce branches is helpful in avoiding this damage.

56 **Holly Leaf Miner,** *Phytomyza ilicis*

Winding tunnels and whitish blisters on the leaves are indications of the presence of the larvae of this little fly. The mined leaves turn yellow and often fall to the ground by the end of the summer. An attack causes the plant to secrete ethylene which poisons it and any leaves with larvae should be picked and destroyed early in the summer. The fly is active in May and June and insecticides can successfully be applied at this time.

57 Honey Fungus, *Armillaria mellea*

This most serious fungus disease will attack both deciduous trees and conifers. Initially the tree loses its healthy appearance, fewer leaves or needles are produced and it gradually dies. From the roots nearest the surface and the lower part of the stem clumps of yellowish, honey-coloured, mushroom-like fruiting bodies are produced. If a part of the bark is removed, white-streaked fungus bodies can also be seen against the wood. Another characteristic sign of the disease are the rhizomorphs—black-brown, coarse and quite tough fungus 'roots' which are found under the bark on the trunk and main roots. In a severe attack the inner part of the wood becomes a pulpy mass, which may even assume a phosphorescent tinge. Even though the fruiting bodies produce millions of spores which are carried by the wind to infect healthy trees, it is usually the rhizomorphs which transmit the disease from one tree to another through the roots in the soil. The most susceptible trees are Norway Spruce (*Picea abies*), *Thuja*, Junipers (*Juniperus*), Thorns (*Crataegus*) and Poplars (*Populus*), while the Silver Fir (*Abies alba*) is quite resistant. There is really no method of control except to completely destroy infected trees, including the stump and as many roots as possible. The fungus will not always infect neighbouring trees, it will sometimes come to a halt after killing one tree, but every precaution should be taken once a tree is attacked.

58 Douglas Fir Aphid, *Gilletteella cooleyi*

The wax-covered small insects can sometimes make the needles appear all white, but the damage caused is insignificant if the trees have a sufficient water supply. There is a host change between the Douglas Fir (*Pseudotsuga*) and some spruces (see no. 7).

59 Frost damage on Japanese Cedar, *Cryptomeria*

Where this species of tree is grown at its northernmost limit and there are fluctuations of temperature during the winter, frost damage will occur. This becomes visible in the spring when large areas of the branches become brown with dead needles. Japanese Cedar will only escape frost damage if the winter temperature is constant. Affected branches should be pruned in the spring.

60 Variegation in *Thujopsis dolobrata*

A great number of conifers have a variegation of bluish and yellow-green needles but very few, other than *Thujopsis dolobrata*, have white and cream variegations. This is an inherited phenomenon.

61 Privet Hawk Moth, *Sphinx ligustri*

One of the biggest and prettiest of the night-flying moths, it has picturesque caterpillars which grow up to 10 cm long and eat leaves and shoots. They usually only appear in small numbers and the damage can be controlled by collecting the caterpillars.

62 Tortrix Moth, *Cacoecia rosana*

The yellowish or green caterpillars of this moth often crawl backwards, and when disturbed will lower themselves to the ground on a thread. The caterpillar weaves the leaves together to form a small tent and then feeds on the leaves from the inside. Treatment with chemicals is rarely necessary since the damage to healthy bushes is usually very slight. If a number are noticed it is best to cut them off and burn them. The Privet Moth (*Coriscium cuculipennellum*) can cause similar symptoms of attack.

63 Leaf Aphid, *Aphis ligustri*

This aphid may appear in such numbers that the leaves curl and the growth of the shoots is severely checked. When there are just a few they can be washed off with a jet of water, otherwise spraying with an insecticide will be necessary. The variety *Ligustrum ovalifolium* is resistant to attack from this pest.

64 Lilac Moth, *Gracillaria syringella*

A small variegated night-flying moth which lays her eggs during May and June on the lower surfaces of the lilac leaves and occasionally on *Ligustrum* and *Deutzia*. The caterpillars eat large, round mines in the leaves. When present in large numbers the appearance of the plants can be spoilt and also quite a lot of the foliage is shed. A second generation in the latter part of the summer may increase the damage. Insecticide treatment is effective when the caterpillars are very small. Alternatively infested leaves can be removed and burnt to reduce the threat of future infestation.

65 Thorn Powdery Mildew, *Podosphaera oxyacanthae*

An attack by this fungus will cover the tips of shoots and the young leaves with a grey-white layer. It starts as a few spots which later merge and cause a check in shoot growth, sometimes growth is completely stopped. The disease only attacks Thorn (*Crataegus*) species. Spraying with a suitable fungicide at the first signs of the disease will prevent its spread.

66 Thorn Aphid, *Ovatus crataegarius*

Leaves and shoot tips of the Thorn (*Crataegus*) can be infested by this insect which causes damage both by sucking the plant juices and by depositing the honey-dew on which the sooty mould fungus grows. Growth is reduced and the plant has an unpleasant appearance, although older trees do not really suffer. Young and new plants can be damaged and suffer a severe growth check. On such plants an infestation is best controlled with a suitable insecticide.

67 Fireblight, *Erwinia amylovora*

This is a devastating bacterial disease, known in N. America for over two hundred years but in Europe only for some fifteen years. Apart from Apple (*Malus*) and Pear (*Pyrus*) the most common trees and bushes attacked are Hawthorn (*Crataegus*), Cotoneaster, Pyracantha, Whitebeam

(*Sorbus*), Quince (*Chaenomles* and *Cydonia*), and ornamental *Malus spp.* When fireblight attacks thorns the leaves become yellow, then brown and whole branches die, but it is seldom that the entire tree dies, as with Pears (*Pyrus*). The tree or hedge will often look as though it has been damaged by fire. In most countries it is a notifiable disease and infected trees or bushes must be dug out and burnt. No effective control measures have yet been found and it is therefore vital to prevent its spread by phytosanitary measures, for example if the disease is suspected, pruning implements should be dipped in disinfectant before pruning healthy material. It is a more common disease in orchards than gardens, but the Hawthorn (*Crataegus*) in gardens can be an important source of infection.

68 Gall Midge, *Dasyneura crataegi*
This insect is probably the most noticeable of all those which live on the Hawthorn (*Crataegus*), since the 2–3 mm-long, whitish larvae produce the so-called thorn roses on the tips of the shoots. Although the hawthorn bushes rarely suffer any real damage, a severe attack can spoil the appearance in the late summer when these thorn roses wither. In areas where Fireblight (no. 67) is common, there is the danger that the disease may enter through the small scars left by the larvae. It is therefore preferable to pick off and burn any thorn roses as soon as they are noticed.

69 Leaf Sucker, *Psylla pyrisuga*
At the beginning of the summer leaf suckers can appear in large numbers on Hawthorn (*Crataegus*) and with their sucking stunt the growth of the leaves and shoots. The yellow-green, winged insects, some 2 mm long, and their slightly smaller nymphs or larvae usually rest on the lower surfaces of the leaves. When present in large numbers insecticide treatment is justified.

70 Thorn Rust, *Gymnosporangium clavariaeforme*
This disease produces small brown spots, which later develop into swellings, on the leaves and shoots and sometimes on the flowers and fruits. The most serious effect of this is that the shoots become deformed and bend sideways. Juniper (*Juniperus*) (no. 41) may also be attacked. The disease can be prevented by spraying with a specific fungicide in the early summer.

71 Lime Red Spider Mite, *Tetranychus tiliae*
Like most mites this one is minute, barely half a millimetre long. The colour is green-yellow, but the overwintering female is red. The eggs are laid on the leaves in the spring and the many generations which develop during the summer smother the stems and branches with a shining web. The leaves turn yellow and fall as early as August. Although the Large Leaved Lime (*Tilia grandifolia*) and *Tilia platyphyllos* can be severely attacked, the Small Leaved Lime (*Tilia parvifolia*) and *Tilia cordata* appear resistant, and these two species should be grown in areas where this mite is common.

72 Lime Gall Mite, *Eriophyes tetratrichus*

This mite makes small, ball-shaped galls, with very narrow openings, on the undersurface of leaves. Inside the galls there is a close felt-like surface which the plant has been made to produce. A large number of colourless mites live inside the gall, crawl around and suck the cell tissues, but the damage caused is insignificant.

73 Gall Mite, *Eriophyes tiliae*

Another species of mite found on Limes (*Tilia*) which produce long, horn-like galls but do no damage to the trees.

74 Gall Mite, *Eriophyes liosoma*

This is a 'mite-felt' producing species. With their stiletto-shaped mouths the mites inject small amounts of an unknown substance into the leaves which makes the normal smooth-surface cells produce long, juicy hairs on which the mites live. On healthy trees no real damage is caused.

75 Leaf Wasp, *Eriocampoides annulipes*

The centimetre-long, greenish larva of this wasp feeds on the lower surface of the leaves. It can be identified particularly by its habit of just eating the fleshy part of the leaf and leaving the cuticle or skin behind. It is also common on Oak (*Quercus*). If treatment is essential, as may be the case on newly planted trees, an insecticide should be applied while the larval stage is still present.

76 San José Oyster-shell Scale, *Quadraspidiotus perniciosus*

In many countries of the world this is a real pest on a number of garden plants as it feeds not only on the leaves and fruits but also on the twigs and branches. The symptoms are clusters of small round spots. Inside each is a female insect under a greyish round scale up to 2 mm in diameter. They can become so numerous that the branches appear to be completely covered. In some countries it is a notifiable pest and government experts will take the necessary control measures. Some of the newer insecticides are quite effective against this scale and thorough spraying will usually produce effective control.

77 Birch Leaf Roller, *Deporaus betulae*

Normally, this small black weevil, about half a centimetre long, appears only on Birch (*Betula*) and Alder (*Alnus*). During the summer eggs are laid on the leaves which then curl up and hide the young larvae inside. Although the larvae feed until the leaves are tattered and wilted the damage is not of any real importance and treatment is unnecessary. On small garden trees the curled leaves can be picked off and burnt with the larvae inside.

78 Silver Green Leaf Weevil, *Phyllobius argentatus*

Most of the *Phyllobius spp.* of weevils are a metallic green or brownish colour and about half a centimetre long. They will often appear in large numbers on Birch (*Betula*) and other deciduous trees early in the summer and feed on the leaves. This feeding only lasts a couple of weeks and rarely causes any harm to the trees. If young garden trees are attacked the weevils can be shaken down onto a cloth spread below the tree during the evening when they are inactive. They can then be collected and destroyed.

79 Witches Broom, *Taphrina betulina*

During the winter, when there are no leaves on the trees to obstruct the view, dense masses of shoots, up to half a centimetre in diameter, can sometimes be seen on older birch trees. Over the years this has been produced by a very large number of short shoots having developed on a side branch. It has the appearance of a bird's nest, and the old superstition was that it had been made by witches. In fact it is a fungus disease which grows inside the larger branches. There is no control for the disease. To prevent the appearance of the tree being spoilt, the mass of shoots can be cut away.

80 Leaf Miner, *Agromyza alni-betulae*

This is one of the fly species whose larvae live between the upper and lower surfaces of the leaf where they make both narrow twisting mines and large round mines. The illustrated species starts off with a narrow mine and ends with a round one. If this is opened the maggot-like larva, only a few mm long, will be found inside. Healthy growing trees are not damaged by the attack.

81 Leaf Aphid, *Euceraphis punctipennis*

This species, together with a couple of other species, can be extremely numerous on Birch (*Betula*) in June and July without usually causing any damage to healthy trees. Their honey-dew can be a nuisance and produces the usual sooty mould. Chemical spraying is usually unnecessary, except perhaps on newly planted small trees, although a thorough drenching with water often helps.

82 Birch Looper Moth, *Biston betularius*

An interesting moth because there are two distinct colour types: one very light with black speckled wings, the other dark all over. This latter is said to have spread in urban areas where it has assumed the darker colour because the trees are coated with dirt from factories, and its colour is then greater protection from birds. The larvae eat the foliage but rarely cause any real damage.

83 Birch Rust, *Melampsoridium betulinum*

On the lower surface of birch leaves small yellow-orange spots may develop and when they are sufficiently numerous they merge together to form a continuous layer. The disease does not appear until later in the summer, when the damage it causes is not serious. Control measures are almost impossible and really unnecessary.

84 Gall Mite, *Eriophyes brevitarsus*

This species is almost microscopic and forms a felt-like cover on the lower surface of the leaves which is first a whitish yellow and then later becomes brownish. The tiny, oblong, whitish mites can be seen among this felt with the aid of a good magnifying glass. Both Birch (*Betula*) and Alder

(*Alnus*) may be attacked but the damage is of no consequence on healthy trees.

85 Buff-tip Moth, *Phalera bucephala*

This moth is extremely well camouflaged when resting on the stem of a birch tree. The larvae are rather harmful, partly because they are voracious feeders and partly because they appear in such large numbers that they can practically strip the leaves from many deciduous trees, including Birch (*Betula*) and Alder (*Alnus*). Suitable insecticides are effective against the young caterpillars, but spraying is sometimes unnecessary in gardens where collecting the caterpillars is a possibility.

86 Gall Wasp, *Diplolepis longiventris*

These conspicuous galls can often be seen on the lower surfaces of oak leaves and may be up to 1 cm in diameter. The whitish larva which lives inside the gall, develops into a so called female generation which reproduces by parthenogenesis (virgin birth). A male–female generation develops in grey-green galls on the end buds. The damage caused is insignificant.

87 Oak Gall Wasp, *Diplolepis quercus-folii*

The oak has several gall wasps, and this one produces large galls of up to 2 cm in diameter. These oak apples are often red at first becoming brown later. In some years they are so numerous that branches can be weighed down, yet no damage seems to be done to the trees. A female generation emerges from these galls (no. 86), while the male–female generation develops in much smaller, violet bud galls.

88 Gall Wasp, *Neuroterus albipes*

The disc galls of this species on Oak (*Quercus*) contain the female generation (no. 86), while the male–female generation larvae form 2 mm-long green or yellowish galls on the edge of the leaves. Neither this, nor any of the other gall wasps on oak, appear to have any effect on the growth of the trees.

89 Oak Powdery Mildew, *Microsphaera quercina*

Initially showing as greyish spots, this powdery mildew can quickly develop into a greyish film on the leaves and young shoots, and can then affect shoot development. The attack can be very severe in the summer when the oak trees produce the very soft 'water shoots'. Young trees can be protected by spraying mildew-specific fungicides, larger trees which are difficult to spray are better able to withstand an attack.

90 Leaf Spot, *Gloeosporium umbrinellum*

The brown areas on the leaves are due to a fungus disease. They are not, as may be thought, a physiological disorder due, perhaps, to unsuitable climatic conditions or poor soil. The disease is uncommon on young trees and as far as older trees are concerned it does little damage and the collection of all diseased leaves in the autumn is hardly feasible.

91 Elm Leaf Aphid, *Schizoneura ulmi*

This aphid is also called the Red-currant Root Aphid because of its host change from the Elm (*Ulmus*) to the various *Ribes* species such as redcurrant, gooseberry and black-currant. In the early part of the summer colonies of greenish, wingless aphids develop inside the curled elm leaves. In mid-summer winged aphids emerge and fly to *Ribes* where they reproduce, and this generation travels to the roots where they feed. Late in the autumn another winged genera-tion moves back to the elm where overwintering takes place in the egg phase. The damage is rarely severe enough to justify treatment.

92 Dutch Elm Disease, *Ceratostomella ulmi*

Dutch elm disease causes the leaves first to turn yellow or light brown and then to wither and fall, giving the tree the appearance of dying back. If branches or shoots are cut, a brownish stain, which is caused by the fungus, can be seen inside. The disease is transmitted from tree to tree by the Elm Bark Beetles (*Scolytus spp.*) which carry the spores of the fungus from infected to healthy trees. Even large trees are killed by the disease. In many countries, including the U.K., there has been legislation concerning the disease and action can be taken to fell and clear diseased trees. Control over a wide area is extremely difficult, but valuable isolated trees can be protected by treatment with an insecticide from May onwards to kill any beetles, and by annual injection of the tree with a systemic fungicide. This treatment is expensive but appears to be very successful. It also seems that over periods of years the fungus passes through quiescent phases when there is little or no disease and then a virulent strain appears for a few years. It is only during the latter that the expensive treatments are essential.

93 Coral Spot Canker, *Nectria cinnabarina*

This disease is not especially con-nected with the Elm (*Ulmus*), but wherever dead or withered branches of deciduous trees are left lying on the ground the pale red or vermilion spore bodies, 1–2 mm in size, of this disease may develop. The fungus in this manner contributes to the decomposition of the wood. It can, however, also penetrate living wood through wounds produced by pruning and from there develop until it kills even strong, main branches. As a prevention, all dead branches and prunings should be removed and burnt and all pruning cuts treated with a wound sealant.

94 Lackey Moth, *Malacosoma neustria*

Sometimes, early in summer, whole sections of the branches of Elm (*Ulmus*), Apple (*Malus*) and other deciduous trees are completely stripped of leaves by colonies of variegated caterpillars. These are very social and always keep together. They will often seek mutual protection within a tent-like web, and when they have stripped a tree they will migrate in a group down to the ground and then along to another tree. The ochreous moth flies in the late summer, and lays her eggs on the twigs in the characteristic collar or cuff around the twig. The eggs hatch the following spring. The egg masses can be cut off if they are discovered or, alternatively, the newly hatched caterpillars can be sprayed with insecticide. The large caterpillars are difficult to kill with the usual sprays.

95 Elm Leaf Hopper, *Typhlocyba ulmi*

If the leaves become discoloured and take on a light, variegated appearance, the cause can usually be found on the lower leaf surfaces where large numbers of small leaf hoppers, a few millimetres long, will be feeding. If disturbed they can be seen to run. The damage they do is of no real importance.

96 Beech Scale, *Cryptococcus fagi*

Pieces of 'wool' can sometimes be seen on the bark of beech trees in the summer. These are, in reality, legless aphids 1 mm long, covered in white waxy threads and with their sucking mouth parts firmly attached to the bark. The aphid overwinters as the egg. In the spring the small, reddish larvae, which have legs, find suitable places in the bark where they soon develop into adults. Only trees in a poor growing condition are seriously attacked. If the growing conditions are improved the scale soon disappears.

97 Beech Gall Midge, *Hartigiola annulipes*

Small hard galls on beech leaves, which are first whitish and then later brown, are caused by the larvae of this midge. The damage is usually insignificant.

98 Gall Midge, *Mikiola fagi*

The adult midge is about 2 mm long, flies in spring and lays its eggs on the upper surface of beech leaves. The larvae make pointed reddish galls, which may be as tall as 1 cm. These galls gradually loosen themselves and fall to the ground. No damage is done to the trees.

99 Gall Mite, *Eriophyes nervisequus*

This is one of the species which forms the so-called 'mite felt', which is produced by small, greyish deposits on the leaf surface. The tiny, oblong, whitish mite, which can be seen with a good magnifying glass, lives in between these fine felt-like threads. In the case of very large numbers the leaves may curl and whither. Spraying with sulphur can be used as a preventive, or an approved acaricide will control an outbreak on small trees. Large trees do not normally suffer any real damage from this pest.

100 Gall Mite, *Eriophyes sp.*

There are other *Eriophyes* species which will cause a similar type of 'mite felt' to that described in no. 99.

101 Beech Leaf Miner, *Orchestes fagi*

The adult weevil is only 2–3 mm long, but sometimes appears in very large numbers when the beech leaves are opening. Their feeding then produces small circular holes in the leaves which become larger as the leaves grow. The larvae make winding mines in the leaves which terminate in a large mine at the tip or edge of the leaf. Only in the case of a very large infestation is it worthwhile taking control measures, and then an insecticide should be used as the leaves are expanding.

102 Beech Leaf Aphid, *Phyllaphis fagi*

This aphid, about 2 mm long, is really green but because of the layer of wax covering it, it appears to be white. It can multiply so rapidly early in the summer that the shoots and leaves can be completely covered with the colonies. Newly planted hedges can be seriously damaged and should be protected by spraying with an insecticide in May and June if the aphid is present. Usually natural control takes over later but on young bushes the damage may have been done by then.

103 Gall Midge, *Helicomyia saliciperda*

The eggs of this midge are laid on the bark of two- to three-year-old branches during May and June when the adult is actively flying. The larvae bore their way through the bark and into the wood so that after repeated attacks the bark and wood cracks and becomes frayed. This stops the supply of plant nutrients so that the branch above the damage wilts and dies. Such damage can spoil trees like Willow (*Salix*). If necessary the attacked branches and twigs can be sawn off and destroyed, thus killing the overwintering larvae. There are other gall midges which attack the willow, some forming galls on the leaves and the tips of the shoots (willow roses).

104 Leaf Beetle, *Phyllodecta vulgatissima*

This is one of several leaf beetles which, with their larvae, feed on the leaves of willow and poplar trees. They have no effect on the growth of large trees, but if they are seen on young trees in large numbers they should be shaken down and collected. Heavy infestations of larvae can be successfully sprayed with a suitable insecticide provided they are still fairly small.

105 Leaf Wasp, *Pteronus salicis*

The distinctive larvae are very greedy feeders and can completely strip all the foliage from young trees in the summer. Small infestations do little damage but, if necessary, the larvae can either be shaken from the trees or sprayed with insecticide.

106 Leopard Moth, *Zeuzera pyrina*

The wing span of the female moth is nearly 7 cm compared with the male's 4 cm. The elegant spotting on the female's wings give the species its name. They fly at night during July and August when the eggs are laid on the bark of deciduous trees, including fruit trees. The larvae bore into branches and shoots, and the tunnels can cause the branch to die. The larvae, yellow with black spots, take two years to develop and become up to 6 cm long. They are extremely difficult to control, the only feasible method is to inject some woodworm fluid into the hole and seal it up.

107 Stem-borer Weevil, *Cryptorrhynchus lapathi*

This fairly large weevil is about 7 mm long. It makes small holes in the bark of Willow (*Salix*) and Elm (*Ulmus*), and occasionally in Poplar (*Populus*) and Birch (*Betula*). The damage by the adults is insignificant compared to that done by the larvae, which bore tunnels in the branches and shoots and often cause them to wither and die. The only method of control is to prune infected branches and burn them, thus destroying the larvae inside.

108 Gall Wasp, *Pontania capreae*
The eggs are laid on willow leaves and the emerging larvae enter the leaves, forming bubble-like blisters in which they develop. These galls have no harmful effect on the trees, but if there are a lot it is preferable to pick them off and burn them.

109 Willow Mildew, *Uncinula salicis*
The disease shows up as grey-white spots on leaves and shoot tips in the middle of the summer. Growth is temporarily halted, but willows are vigorous growers and such a set-back is hardly noticeable. Weaker growing varieties which have been pruned hard and could therefore be really checked in growth should be sprayed with a suitable fungicide.

110 Willow Scale, *Chionaspis salicis*
Oblong, oblique whitish scales are formed on the bark of Willow (*Salix*), Poplar (*Populus*) and several other deciduous trees. The scales can be so dense that the bark appears to shine, yet they do not seem to do any real harm to the tree.

111 Rust, *Melampsora spp.*
This fungus shows as yellow to yellow-orange pustules on the lower surface of the leaves which they can cover so completely that the leaves, and even the whole shoot, may lose its green colour. There are several species of rust, and they also attack Poplar (*Populus*). Treatment is unnecessary.

112 Willow Scab, *Fusicladium saliciperdum*
Weeping willow is particularly susceptible to scab. Both leaves, shoots and branches are attacked. Soon after the leaves open damage from the previous year is visible, either as dead branches or branches with only a few leaves on them. The fungus grows into the bark where greyish, rough sections of a few millimetres to 2 cm in length occur. These interfere with sap movement to the shoot tips so that wilting occurs and branches die. During the summer, small brown spots may also be seen on the leaves. Although the fungus prefers humid conditions, it can also thrive in dry, exposed sites. Since the weeping willow grows vigorously every year and control of the fungus is extremely difficult, it is best to prune all diseased branches just after leaf emergence in the spring.

113 Poplar Scab, *Fusicladium radiosum*
Although poplar scab is closely related to willow scab (no. 112), there are certain differences in the symptoms of attack. In addition to the leaf spots in the middle of summer, young shoots will completely wither away and the infection on the branches is not so obvious. Spraying during the

early summer can have some effect, otherwise all infected shoots should be pruned and burnt. It can often happen that certain trees in a row do not have the disease and any cuttings that are required should be taken from these resistant trees.

114 Mosaic Virus Disease
This can make the leaves a variegated yellow-green from soon after leaf burst until the end of the summer. The tree does not appear to suffer any damage, but if gardeners consider that it is no longer attractive then it must be removed as there is no cure for the disease.

115 Poplar Canker, *Dothichiza populea*
Initially developing as brown discoloured patches on the trunk and larger branches, the canker will form larger wounds, girdle the stem and kill the branch above the infection. In serious cases the branches must be pruned. If the infection is noticed early enough it can be stopped with a fungicide containing a wound-healing preparation.

116 Goat Moth, *Cossus cossus*
One of the largest of the night-flying moths, the Goat Moth has red caterpillars which can be up to 8–9 cm long. These tunnel in the trunks of various deciduous trees, especially Poplar (*Populus*) and Willow (*Salix*). Young trees can be so severely damaged by this tunnelling that they will snap off in a storm, while older trees lose their bark over the affected parts of the trunk. To save valuable trees some woodworm liquid can be put into the holes which should then be sealed with grafting wax. A willow hedge can be pruned annually so that the new branches are too thin to be attacked by the caterpillar.

117 Leaf Aphid, *Pemphigus spirothecae*
This aphid produces rather striking purse-shaped galls on the leaf stalks or petioles of the leaves of Poplars (*Populus*), which also have other species of aphids such as *Pemphigus bursarius*. Later in the summer the winged generation leaves the galls and flies to Lettuce (*Lactuca*) where a wingless generation emerges and feeds on the roots. A closely related species, *P. dauci*, produces galls in the centre of the leaves and these have the Carrot (*Daucus*) as their alternate host. The poplar trees do not suffer from the aphids, it is the latter's feeding on vegetable crops that is most serious. If there are vegetables close to attacked poplar trees the trees should be sprayed with a suitable insecticide to prevent migration to the vegetables.

118 Satin Moth, *Stilpnotia salicis*
About every fourth year there appears to be an outbreak of caterpillars and the variegated larvae can completely defoliate Poplar (*Populus*) and Willow (*Salix*) trees during May and June. The larvae pass into the pupal stage in a tent-like web and a couple of weeks later the pretty white moths can be seen swarming around the trees laying their eggs on the bark. Although the damage may appear serious, older trees do not seem to suffer ill effects, but younger trees should be sprayed with an insecticide as soon as the caterpillars are seen.

119 Poplar Moth, *Amorpha populi*
A large night moth whose caterpillars
will eat the leaves and young shoots.
At times it will also attack Apple
(*Malus*), but it is only rarely a pest.

120 Eyed Hawk Moth, *Smerinthus
ocellatus*
The larvae of this beautiful night
moth can eat the leaves and shoots
of Poplar (*Populus*) and certain other
deciduous trees in a similar manner
to the caterpillars of the Poplar
Moth (no. 119).

121 Poplar Blister, *Taphrina
aurea*
This fungus disease does not become
apparent until late in the summer.
Then, grooves about 1 cm in
diameter, which become yellow, are
formed on the lower surface of the
leaves with corresponding grey-green
blisters on the upper surface. The
disease is only seen on Poplar (*Populus*) and will cause leaf shedding, but
it rarely harms the trees as only a few
leaves are usually infected.

122 Poplar Leaf Beetle, *Melasoma
populi*
This 1 cm long beetle, and its black-
spotted larva, can skeletonise the
poplar's leaves during the early
summer but they seldom cause any
real damage to the trees. If present
on new plantings they can be shaken
off and collected.

123 Leaf Beetle, *Melasoma aeneum*
The habits and life cycle of this beetle
closely resemble those of no. 122. It,
too, does not cause any damage.

124 Willow Leaf Beetle,
Gallerucella lineola
This beetle is similar to the two
previous ones, nos. 122 and 123, and
causes very little damage.

125 Silver Leaf Disease, *Stereum
purpureum*
First this fungus causes a single branch
to lose its fresh colour, and then
gradually the whole tree as the leaves
take on a grey-green tinge which
becomes grey or silver-grey. Some
leaves will become brown, growth
stops, branches will die, and the whole
tree slowly deteriorates. A white, hard
fruit body from the fungus often
appears at about soil level attached to
the trunk. The fungus lives in the
wood of the tree and is never found
in the leaves. The silver colour is
caused by toxins produced in the
sap stream by the fungus and carried
to the leaves. A comparison of
healthy and diseased branches will
show up mild attacks. There is no
treatment, diseased trees must be
completely dug up and destroyed.
Not only Poplar (*Populus*) but a large
number of other deciduous trees can
be attacked, particularly *Prunus spp.*
The so-called False Silver Leaf has a
similar appearance, but is not
caused by a pathogen and disappears
after a couple of years. The leaf discolouration is physiological and is
caused by nutrient imbalance in the
tree. It often appears after hard
pruning, when the ratio of root to
shoot is out of balance.

126 Poplar Leaf Spot, *Marssonina
populi*
Black-brown spots, a couple of millimetres in size, are produced on the

leaves. In serious cases the leaves fall off, but if necessary the disease can be prevented by fungicide sprays during the summer.

127 Blue Headed Owl Moth,
Episema coeruleocephala

This is really the name of the caterpillar, as the moth is usually associated with the various fruit tree caterpillars. The moth flies in the autumn, the eggs overwinter on the trees and in early spring the young caterpillars begin to eat the leaves and buds, usually of Poplar (*Populus*), Thorn (*Crataegus*) and fruit trees. The feeding stops fairly early in the summer and it is only on fruit trees that treatment is usually necessary.

128 Rowan Rust, *Gymnosporangium corniferum*

Small spots will develop on the leaves of Rowan (*Sorbus*) during the summer. These are red-yellow on the upper surface, while the lower surface of the leaves are thickened and brown-grey. The disease has a host change on Juniper (*Juniperus*) where it appears as small yellow pustules on the needles. The damage is usually of no consequence to either host.

129 Gall Mite, *Eriophyes goniothorax sorbeus*

This minute spider forms felt-like spots on the leaves which are first white and then turn brown. With the aid of a good magnifying glass it is possible to see the mites moving among the hairs on which they live. The attack is of no importance to healthy trees.

130 Rowan Mosaic Virus Disease

This mosaic disease is largely confined to the small veins of the leaves which it shows up as greyish-green flecks, whereas most other forms of mosaic disease are yellow-green. The Common Rowan (*Sorbus aucuparia*) is the most susceptible to attack. There is no treatment.

131 Tar Spot Disease, *Rhytisma acerinum*

This disease appears in the middle of the summer as black spots with a yellow edge, 12 cm in size, and as many as ten per leaf. The damage done to the plant is very small and prevention or treatment is unnecessary. The disease is found on Common Maple (*Acer pseudoplatanus*) but rarely on other species of *Acer*.

132 Gall Mite, *Eriophyes macrochelus*

Like most mite species this one is difficult to see with the naked eye. Like the closely related species (no. 129) it forms felt-like spots on the lower surface of the leaves of Rowan (*Sorbus*) which can also be seen on the upper surface as small bumps. Normally the trees do not suffer any damage from an attack.

133 Mildew, *Uncinula circinata*

This disease appears as an off-white covering on the leaves and shoot tips. Growth stops and if the hedge is cut it then attacks the new, soft growth. It is worst on Hedge Maple (*Acer campestris*). The bushes should be protected by spraying at least twice during the summer with a mildew-specific fungicide.

134 Natural white and red variegation on Kolomikta Vine, *Actinidia kolomikta*

The variegation shows first on the outer third or half of the leaf, which becomes white to white-grey as though attacked by mildew. This later changes to a bright red. This development of colour is natural and very much appreciated by some gardeners.

135 Red Currant Blister Aphid, *Cryptomyzus ribis*

This aphid is the cause of the wrinkling with red and yellow spots, which spoils the appearance of the leaves of many *Ribes* varieties. Black and red currant bushes are particularly susceptible to attack. It causes the leaves to wilt early and drop at least one month before the normal time. If this happens two years in succession, control measures should be taken and an insecticide sprayed in the spring soon after the aphids have emerged from the overwintering eggs.

136 Physiological branch distortion—fasciation

If one or two branches are abnormally broad and flat, there has usually been a fusion of two or three branches in what is known as fasciation. This word is taken from the Latin *fasces*, meaning a bundle of branches. The distortion is caused by abnormal cell division in a bud. If the distorted branch is cut off the rest of the bush grows quite normally. Fasciation is most common in forsythia but can also occur in many plants and flowers.

137 Bunching Bacterial Disease, *Corynebacterium fascians*

Neglected, old bushes growing in the shade may develop bunches of very short shoots varying in length from a few millimetres to a couple of centimetres. A crack in the branches may also be caused by the distortion arising from this bacterial disease. Although it cannot be cured it will disappear if the bushes are thoroughly pruned, and this, at the same time, will stimulate the production of flower producing shoots.

138 Vine Weevil, *Otiorrhynchus sulcatus*

In addition to rhododendron this 1 cm-long weevil and its larvae will damage a whole range of valuable garden plants including azalea, begonia, primula, strawberry (*Fragaria*), etc. The damage caused in glasshouses is even greater than outdoors and it is therefore also called the glasshouse weevil. It can nearly always be found around older rhododendron bushes where the characteristic feeding on the leaves shows as notches around the edges. The weevil is only active at night and so can only be found on the bushes after dark. The larvae are in the soil around the bushes where they feed on the bark at the top of the roots and base of the stem. They are whitish, squat larvae and can do considerable damage if present in fair numbers. The weevils are unable to fly and can often be collected by placing small heaps of sawdust under upturned flower pots. New plants should always be checked for adults and larvae. Sprinkling insecticide powder around the base of the bushes will also control them.

139 Larvae of the Vine Weevil,
Otiorrhynchus sulcatus
These larvae can often be seen in numbers around the roots of many species of plants (see no. 138).

140 Winter damage
Rhododendrons can, like other evergreen, non-deciduous plants, be damaged during the winter by temperature fluctuations because, during milder spells, the evaporation from the leaves cannot be compensated by the uptake of water from the roots which are often in frozen soil. The result is a type of drought scorch. By placing spruce or pine branches in between the susceptible plants it is often possible to avoid the worst of this damage as they keep the temperature more even and reduce fluctuations.

141 Rhododendron Bug,
Stephanitis rhododendri
By sucking on the leaves, these bugs produce a yellow spotted upper surface and a dirty looking, discoloured lower surface to the leaves, causing them to curl. The adults have lace-like wings, hence their name of lace bugs, and are 3–4 mm long. They lay their eggs along the central vein on the lower surface of the leaf and the following spring produce colonies of rather flat larvae. If the infestation is heavy it is probably advisable to spray the infested bushes with a suitable insecticide, taking care to see that the lower surfaces of the leaves are covered with spray.

142 Rhododendron Whitefly,
Dialeurodes chittendeni
These small, 2 mm-long insects are not true flies. They are related to aphids and suck the lower surfaces of leaves so that they become yellow. Most damage is, however, caused by the scale-like larvae which emerge from the eggs also laid on the lower leaf surfaces. Spraying with a suitable insecticide is only essential if the infestation is very heavy.

143 Gall or False Bloom,
Exobasidium vaccinii
This fungus is only found on rhododendrons and azaleas where it can cause the buds to come to a complete standstill. The early symptoms are light brown irregular growths on the young leaves and shoot tips, and at times also on the flower petals. There is no control except to cut off the infected branches.

144 Wilting of Heather,
Rhizoctonia solani
The first symptoms of an attack by this disease are a few shoots producing yellow needles, but these later become brown and wilt. The initial symptoms are very similar to those produced by unsuitable growing conditions and it is not until the brown discolouration is obvious that the two conditions can be separated. Cutting off the infected shoots will sometimes stop the disease, otherwise the plants have to be removed and burnt. If heather is being replanted in the same spot the surrounding soil must be replaced since the fungus is carried over in the soil.

145 Comma Scale, *Lepidosaphes ulmi*

These dark brown, comma-shaped scales may be up to 4 mm long. They are found on a large number of different species of deciduous trees and bushes. The insect under the scale is a type of plant bug. The female lays about thirty-five eggs which overwinter and hatch the following spring into mobile larvae. These move around on the bark until, as they become adult, they grow a scale and cease to move around. A small number of scales on a healthy plant do little damage, but a very heavy infestation can kill a plant. The scales can be brushed off during the winter or, alternatively, sprayed with an insecticide early in the summer in order to kill the unprotected larval stage.

146 Grey Monilia Disease, *Monilia laxa*

On the Flowering Almond (*Prunus triloba*) some of the flowers, and the shoots bearing the flowers, will wither away during the latter part of the flowering period and immediately after. It is characteristic of the disease that the damage does not continue, but is limited to these few weeks. If an infected shoot is cut lengthways there is a brown discolouration in the wood in a well-defined streak, as opposed to the general discolouration which occurs with frost damage. Contrary to other fungus diseases the grey monilia enters the plant through the flower. The spores are carried by the wind to the flower where any that settle on the stigma germinate and grow down into the ovary through the style in a similar manner to the pollen. From the fruitlet developing in the ovary the fungus grows out into the wood of the branch. Infected branches should be pruned to reduce the amount of infection for the following year and a fungicide can be used a couple of times at flowering, but no insecticide should be mixed with this spray because of the danger to bees.

147 Firethorn Scab, *Fusicladium pyracanthae*

The disease shows on the upper and lower surfaces of the leaves as brown-green spots, being more prominent on the lower surface. Attacked berries are stopped in their growth because of the brown, corky spots which develop. These can merge to envelop most of the berry, which then shrivels. Control can be obtained by fungicide spraying during the summer, with particular attention to the lower surface of the leaves.

148 Ermine Moth, *Hyponomeuta sp.*

Several different species of the ermine moth may appear on garden plants and the caterpillars can cause considerable damage. *Euonymus*, Rowan (*Sorbus*), various fruit trees and Hawthorn (*Crataegus*) can be more or less smothered by the whitish web built by the caterpillars, and from which they emerge periodically to feed on the leaves. The small moths fly in July and August and lay several clusters of eggs on the bark of the trees. A varnish-like secretion covers the egg masses and also protects the newly hatched caterpillars through the winter. Plants seldom suffer too much from one year's attack, but if it occurs on succeeding years then spraying with insecticide is recommended.

149 Plane Leaf Disease, *Gnomonia veneta*

Brown to brown-black areas appear on the leaves. They are longish and irregular but follow the veins. In its later stages the disease causes leaf shed and in serious cases so many leaves can be lost that it may weaken the tree. Treatment should be applied as soon as possible in the form of several thorough sprayings with a fungicide. The disease does not spread to other species of tree.

150 Mosaic Virus Disease

The illustration shows a common virus disease, the cucumber mosaic, attacking Mezereon (*Daphne mezereum*) in which it produces a coarse, yellow-green leaf variegation followed by loss of leaves and reduced growth. Various trees, bushes and herbaceous plants can be attacked and any perennial plant will act as a source of infection for several years (see no. 203). The attacked plant should be dug up and burnt.

151 Leaf Wasp, *Eriocampoides limacina*

The centimetre-long, slimy larvae of this shiny black wasp can skeletonise the leaves of many deciduous trees as they feed on the upper leaf surface. Usually the attack comes so late in the summer that no real damage is caused.

152 Hare Damage

Twigs and shoots which have been bitten off during the winter usually signify damage by hares, and Broom (*Cytisus*) is one of their favourite plants. Unless the plants are small the damage is not serious, but if hares are a frequent nuisance the use of a suitable repellent will sometimes help.

153 Scale Insect, *Parthenolecanium coryli*

This particular species has quite large scales, up to 5–6 mm long, and is very prolific as the female can lay up to 2,000 eggs. It is not unusual to find older Brooms (*Cytisus*) with branches almost covered by these very arched scales. If the attack is very bad, the most severely damaged branches can be cut off and burnt, others can be brushed with a stiff brush or an insecticide can be tried.

154 Wild Oat Rust, *Puccinia arrhenateri*

Although the disease is not very common on berberis, when it does attack it covers the young shoots, stalks and flower petals, as well as the lower leaf surfaces, with a mass of orange coloured pustules. The edges of the leaves curl upwards, and the flowers do not develop properly. The fungus can overwinter in the branches and a heavy attack can result in the bush deteriorating each year until it dies. It is therefore often best to clear infected bushes before they die.

155 Black Rust, *Puccinia graminis*

This is an extremely serious disease of cereal crops, but is important on berberis since this is its alternate host. In countries where the disease is very serious on cereal crops there are government regulations concerning both wild berberis and the cultivated garden varieties. There are no such restrictions or regulations in the U.K. However, wherever berberis is being cultivated, if the round orange coloured spots of the disease are noticed on the lower surface of the leaves they should either be picked off and burnt or the whole bush dug out and destroyed. At present there is no control available by spraying with fungicides.

156 Earwig, *Forficula auricularia*
Perforated buds and lacerated shoot tips, leaves and flowers indicate the activity of earwigs. It is only active during the night, but can be easily trapped at the foot of the plant in an up-turned flower pot or tray. Alternatively the plant can be sprayed with insecticide if the damage is becoming rather severe. The base of the plant should be thoroughly sprayed.

157 Powdery Mildew, *Erysiphe polygoni*
Since clematis is most often grown on trellises and on the walls of houses the immediate climate is favourable for fungus growth. The mildew can therefore very quickly cover the leaves and buds with its grey-white layer. If a plant becomes infected it will suffer in the following years since the mildew overwinters inside the buds. Spraying with a mildew-specific fungicide should be carried out three or four times during the summer, beginning when the leaves start to appear.

158 Feather or Honeysuckle Moth, *Orneodes hexadactyla*
This moth lays its eggs almost exclusively on Honeysuckle (*Lonicera*)

during the early summer evenings when they can be seen swarming around the plants. The eggs are laid in the flower bud and the young caterpillars feeding inside destroy it, so that it fails to open properly. Only if there are very large numbers of moths is the use of an insecticide spray justified.

159 Leaf Miner, *Phytagromyza hendeliana*
If light coloured, winding tunnels are noticed on the leaves then they are infested with the larvae of the leaf miner fly. The larvae live in the tissue between the upper and lower surfaces of the leaf. Like white maggots in appearance, the larvae inside can become about 2 mm long. The damage is rarely important, but infested leaves are best removed and burnt.

160 Yellow Mosaic Virus Disease
This virus produces yellow discolouration on rose leaves, but the actual appearance of the disease varies very considerably according to the degree of attack. If the virus is very weak, it shows as a yellow streak around the outside of the leaflets, a slightly stronger attack produces small yellow spots all over the leaves, a rather more severe attack produces zig-zag streaks or ring formations, and if the virus is really virulent most of the leaf becomes yellow. It does not attack the flowers, but they become smaller if the bush is severely attacked and it should then be dug up and destroyed.

161   Leaf Cutting Bee, *Megachile centuncularis*

The bees cut circular notches in the edges of the leaves and take the pieces for lining their cylindrical nests. There are other related species which do the same, all of them about a centimetre long. Otherwise these bees are quite harmless, and the bushes do not really suffer from this slight damage.

162   Powdery Mildew of Roses, *Sphaerotheca pannosa*

A whitish layer on the young shoots, leaves, flower buds and petals is the sign of an attack by this fungus, which can restrict growth and reduce the number of flowers. Since the mildew overwinters under the bud scales, hard pruning before bud burst, and the immediate burning of the prunings, will reduce the risk of infection. Summer pruning and excessive amounts of nitrogenous fertiliser also encourage the disease by producing rapid, soft growth. Varieties vary considerably in their susceptibility to mildew, and unless spraying with a mildew specific fungicide can be undertaken regularly, it is better to grow mildew resistant varieties.

163   Rose Tortrix Moth, *Cacoecia rosana*

When leaves and buds are woven together in a web and some feeding damage can be seen, the caterpillars of one of the tortrix moths will be present. They are usually green but can also be yellowish. When disturbed they will lower themselves to the ground on a thread. Since there are several species egg laying continues for most of the summer, so that the 2–3 cm-long caterpillars can be found

over a long period. Removing and burning attacked leaves, or even squeezing them to kill the caterpillars inside, is all that is needed to prevent any damage to the bushes.

164   Small Rose-Leaf Wasp, *Blennocampa pusilla*

Leaves rolled tightly into tubes, with a greenish larva inside, are the result of the small, black leaf wasp laying its eggs on the edge of the leaf about May. The larva is so well protected that chemical treatment is difficult, unless it is carried out before the leaf rolling is well advanced. Otherwise rolled leaves should be removed and burnt.

165   Rose-Hip Fly, *Spilographa alternata*

Late in the summer it is possible to find small pin holes in the ripening rose-hips, accompanied by brown, dented spots. Inside is usually a maggot, whitish and about half a centimetre long, which has reduced the fruit to a brown, rotting pulp. This is the larva of the brownish rose-hip fly which lay their eggs inside the developing fruit in July and August. They are only important in rose varieties, such as *Rosa rugosa* and *R. moyesii*, where the hips are retained for decorative purposes. Attacked hips should be picked and destroyed, and spraying with an insecticide in July will help to prevent an attack.

166   Rose Rust, *Phragmidium mucronatum*

This fungus produces pin-sized, yellow spore growths on the lower surface of the leaves which later become black. The stems and lower leaves can also become covered with an orange coloured layer of the fungus. The disease is only serious when roses are grown in sheltered places, so, for closed-in gardens, some of the many resistant varieties should be chosen. Repeated spraying with an anti-rust fungicide can help, but is not always completely successful in keeping the disease in check on susceptible varieties.

167 Leaf Wasp, *Eriocampoides aethiops*

When the leaves are skeletonised from the upper surface, the trouble can usually be traced to the larvae of this wasp. In large numbers they can harm the bushes and they should be removed or else sprayed with an insecticide when young.

168 Black Spot of Roses, *Diplocarpon rosae*

In some areas this is the most serious disease of roses. Appearing in July, the spots are first brown to red-brown, with a characteristic radiated edge on the older leaves, then they become blackish and the leaves drop off. With a serious attack this spreads up the plant, so that by the end of the season the bush is practically leafless and will have suffered considerable damage to its growth potential for the next year. Repeated sprayings during the summer with a suitable fungicide will keep the disease in check.

169 Rose Root Gall, *Agrobacterium tumefaciens*

This bacterial disease does little damage to plants which are growing well and is not discovered until the bush is dug up. The bacteria enter the roots from the soil and form galls up to 2 cm in thickness. The young galls have a yellowish, smooth surface which changes to brown as they age and become irregular knobs.

170 Garden Chafer Beetle, *Phyllopertha horticola*

These voracious, centimetre-long, brown beetles may appear in large numbers in June and feed on the leaves of roses and many other woody plants in the garden. The damage caused by these beetles is, however, quickly overcome by the plants if they are being well cared for. The larvae can cause quite a lot of damage to lawns, where they feed on the grass roots (no. 182).

171 Rose Aphid, *Macrosiphum rosae*

Nearly 4 mm long, this is one of the largest species of aphids in the garden, and together with one or two other species can cause very considerable damage to the shoots and leaves of roses in the early summer, making future growth very poor. The sooty mould fungus growing on the honey-dew secreted by the aphids also gives the bushes a very unsightly appearance. Soft soap and water to rinse them off was once used, but most insecticides are now very effective against these aphids when thoroughly applied.

172 Cold weather damage

The early leaves often become yellowy and crinkled. This is due to either cold, frosty nights or cold drying winds. The production of further leaves and the general growth is not seriously affected.

173 Gall Wasp, *Rhodites rosae*
Irregular, large reddish galls can sometimes be seen on certain species of roses, particularly the wild ones. These galls are sometimes called Pin Cushion galls. The larvae of this wasp live in the galls which do little or no harm to the plant, unless they become too numerous, when they should be cut off.

174 Rose Leaf Hopper, *Typhlocyba rosae*
Where rose leaves develop pale yellow variegations, colonies of these 3-4 mm-long, light yellow leaf hoppers are usually present on the lower surface where they suck the leaf tissue. The eggs are laid on the small branches so that correct pruning usually keeps the pest under control. Rambling and climbing roses, which are not pruned so much, often suffer more damage and can be sprayed with a suitable insecticide.

175 Rose Stem Borer, *Ardis bipunctata*
If any of the upper shoots are found hanging limply early in the summer the cause is usually the presence of the larva of this stem borer. The yellow-brown larva can be found inside the stem if it is sliced with a sharp knife. Infested shoots are best cut off and burnt as soon as they are noticed.

176 Cold weather damage on *Rosa hugonis*
This can be recognised by red to red-violet dots and small patches on the leaves which develop a few days after the cold weather. No real harm

is done to the plants. Similar damage can be caused by spraying with a copper fungicide since this species of rose is rather susceptible to copper toxicity.

177 Capsid Bug, *Lygus pabulinus*
The feeding of the common capsid bug on shoots and leaves causes a typical deformity which can sometimes seriously inhibit growth. The adult insects are brownish with long legs and are about half a centimetre long. The nymphs or larvae are similar in shape but smaller and greenish. The worst damage will occur in dry weather during the early summer when the bugs can often be shaken out of the buds where they are hiding. If there is a heavy infestation the use of an insecticide may be necessary, otherwise hosing down the bushes with water can help.

178 Leaf Shot-hole Disease, *Stigmina carpophila*
As the name indicates this disease shows as shot-holes in the leaves. These are produced by the fungus, making small, round spots of dead tissue on the young leaves. As the leaves grow these spots are unable to expand and the dead tissue falls out leaving the holes. Fungicide spraying during the summer helps to prevent the disease.

179 Leaf scorch in spring
This type of leaf scorch occurs on older leaves during the spring in areas where the soil is still frozen, but the sun is shining quite strongly. Under these conditions the evaporation from the leaves cannot be replaced by water from the soil and the

leaves turn light brown after a few days. This has no effect on the new leaves which are produced or on the general growth of the bush. The bushes can be protected during the spring with branches of spruce which should not be removed until the needles begin to turn brown as this indicates that the period of danger is over.

180 Cockchafer, *Melolontha melolontha*

The large larvae of this beetle may be up to 5 cm long, and can spoil the lawn by feeding on the roots of the grass, causing it to wither. They can similarly attack annual and perennial flowers, making them wilt and die. Infestations tend to be fairly local and often every four years, mainly because the life cycle takes four years to complete. The beetles fly in the late spring and feed on the leaves of trees, particularly oak and hawthorn, before laying their eggs on the surface of the soil, usually among grass. The larvae emerge in the late summer and enter the soil where they feed on plant roots and develop over the next three years. The larvae make a hollow in the soil before turning into pupae. The adults emerge from these and then over-winter. In the spring they emerge from the soil and begin to fly and feed. Heavy infestations of larvae can be treated with an insecticide watered into the soil and this is best done as soon as the infestation is suspected.

181 Summer Chafer Beetle, *Rhizotrogus solstitialis*

The larvae from this chafer beetle are very similar to those of the cockchafer and the damage they cause is also similar. However, the life cycle is only two years, and the adult emerges about mid-summer. The other difference between the larvae is that those of the summer chafer can crawl on their stomachs while the cockchafer larvae cannot. If treatment is necessary it is the same as for the cockchafer (no. 180).

182 Garden Chafer, *Phyllopertha horticola*

This little chafer beetle is another lawn pest, but as its life cycle is only one year it can cause damage every year. The larvae are 2 cm long, smaller than the cockchafer, but they feed on the roots of all small plants as well as grass. The beetles emerge in early summer and feed on the leaves and buds of various shrubs and trees such as roses and fruit trees, where they even feed on the young fruit. Treatment is similar to that for the other chafer beetles.

183 Blackbird

Although the blackbird consumes large numbers of useful earthworms from the lawn and the flower beds, particularly when they have just been dug, it also eats numbers of harmful insects and therefore probably does more good than harm in the garden. It is also pretty to watch and its song is melodious.

184 Starling

Although a great nuisance in the autumn when it consumes large numbers of berries, throughout the rest of the year the starling feeds mainly on insects, particularly the larvae of the Crane Fly (no. 186).

185 Frit Fly, *Oscinis frit*

The frit fly is 2–3 mm long and black. It lays its eggs on grass plants, preferably in the 2–4-leaf stage. The slim white larvae, which can be up to 7 mm long, feed on the leaves by entering the base of the central shoot. This causes it to turn yellow, wilt and die and this is often followed by the rest of the plant. Newly sown lawns can be completely spoiled if the infestation is heavy. The frit fly has three generations each year and the last one, in August and September, is usually the heaviest. It is therefore advisable to leave the sowing of new lawns until September so that the flies have gone when the grass starts to grow. Attacks are usually worst where large areas of Oats (*Avena*) are grown for harvesting, as this is a main host plant. It is usually too late to treat with an insecticide when the damage is seen, but a spray of insecticide can be applied when the grass is at the four-leaf stage and there is danger of an attack.

186 Crane Fly or Daddy-Long-Legs, *Tipula paludosa* (and other *spp.*)

The grey long-legged females can be seen late in the summer making their low, jumping flight over the lawns. Each time they land they insert their egg-laying tube, or ovipositor, into the soil and leave an egg. The greyish, wrinkled larvae are known as leatherjackets because their skin is so tough. They feed on the grass roots during the autumn and following spring, pupating in the middle of the summer. The pupae work their way to the soil surface where the adults emerge, leaving the empty pupae cases sticking half-way out of the ground. The larvae can be controlled by watering with a suitable insecticide early in the autumn.

187 Seagull

Several types of seagull are among the birds that hunt insects and worms. They can be of great benefit where such large insects as the chafer beetles are concerned, although in their eagerness to reach the larvae they may pick holes in the lawn. On balance, however, it is likely that this damage is less than that caused by the pests.

188 Fairy Rings caused by Fungus

These rings vary from about half a metre in diameter up to five metres. They increase in size each year because the fungi cannot grow in the same soil more than once and therefore move outwards about 15–20 cm each year. The grass becomes greener where the ring was because the fungi mycelium decomposes and releases nitrogen from which the grass benefits. Several species of toadstool fungi can form fairy rings, and although most do not grow very high above ground, the mycelium will go up to a full metre in depth in the soil. Treatment by watering the soil, therefore, has very little effect. The reason why the fungus disappears as suddenly as it appeared is unknown, but until it does go the lawn should be well fertilised and cared for.

189 Greying of grass by Fusarium Disease, *Fusarium nivale*

In areas where lawns are frequently snow covered for long periods during the winter, spots of wilted grass covered by a grey-white layer often appear in the spring. The snow covering enables the fungus to thrive during the winter, so removing the snow during the winter helps the grass withstand the fungus. However, the new growth of grass in the spring is usually healthy without any treatment. It also helps not to leave too much growth of grass during the winter but, if necessary, a suitable fungicide can be sprinkled on the lawn in the late autumn or early spring.

190 Dollar Spot, *Sclerotinia homoeocarpa*

The withered spots caused by the fungus are usually perfectly round but larger than a dollar (2–3 cm). Repeated treatment with a suitable fungicide can help to control the disease, but it is most important to water and fertilise the lawn well.

191 Fungus Disease, *Diachaea leucopoda*

In the distance this disease appears as a white frost on the grass, but on closer observation the greyish, ball-shaped fungus growth can be seen. It grows on the outside of the leaves, apparently living off the air. It usually only appears when the grass growth is poor and the humidity high, so that prevention is to provide plenty of fertiliser and water.

192 Damage after uneven application of fertiliser

Browning of patches or streaks of grass can occur after the hand application of fertiliser and is due to the over-dosage in these patches. If one of the fertilisers that can scorch has been used it is best to water thoroughly immediately afterwards. The grass usually recovers in time, but to avoid this type of damage either use an applicator or a slow-release fertiliser which will not scorch.

193 Ants, *Formicidae*

Ants can be a nuisance, especially around tiles and along paths where they have their nests. They do not cause direct damage to plants, but can loosen the roots with their nesting operations. They love the honey-dew secreted by aphids and will swarm over infested plants, in fact they will often reveal an aphid infestation. If they become too much of a nuisance an ant-killing spray can be used on the nests, or a special lacquer can be painted on to walls and steps where they travel.

194 Scorching caused by dog urine

Dog urine will scorch most plants but it is most obvious on lawns where it appears as yellow, roundish patches. If dogs cannot be kept away the damage can be reduced by frequent watering.

195 Scorching caused by the fungus *Corticium fuciforme*

When grass withers in irregular patches, particularly on older lawns, this fungus is usually the cause. The risk of attack is increased if the lawn is not frequently mown. To check the disease several sprayings of fungicide are necessary.

196 Click Beetle, *Agriotes obscurus*
There are several species of these brown or black beetles, which derive their name from the fact that when placed on their backs they can spring in the air with an audible click and land on their feet. They lay their eggs in the soil, preferably among grass, and the hard, yellow larvae or wire-worms develop over the next four to five years, feeding on the roots of the grass and other plants. Established, well fertilised lawns are rarely damaged, but before sowing a new lawn care should be taken to see that there are very few wireworms present, and if necessary, the soil should be treated.

197 Augusta's Disease
A virus disease which causes brown spots and streaks on the leaves which also twist. It is carried in the bulbs, although it can also be soil-borne. There is no control except to dig up and destroy the plant and bulb.

198 Arabis Mosaic Virus Disease
This is also called 'colour weakening' mosaic disease because the normal colour of the bloom is weakened. In the first year the disease is only seen as a single stripe on a petal, but in succeeding years the stripes increase and broaden with the colour change being to white or yellow. It is some-times suggested that these 'harlequin' varieties should be propagated, but this would be a mistake because of the disease factor and the fact that the

colour pattern changes each year. The disease is also present on the leaves, but the irregular narrow light stripes can only be seen by holding the leaf up and looking through it into a light. There is no treatment for the disease and the whole plant, including the bulb, should be destroyed.

199 Dark Mosaic Virus Disease
The symptoms of this disease are seen less often than those of no. 198 yet it is basically one and the same virus disease. The dark stripes will always go from the tip of the petal to the base. Again there is no cure, plant and bulb should be destroyed.

200 Rattle
This virus disease is seen as dis-colourations on the leaves and flowers, while at the same time the plant is considerably weakened. The disease can infect other plants, such as crocus and hyacinth, so all infected plants must be destroyed. Since infection can also take place through the soil, flower bulbs should not be planted in the soil for five years. (See also nos. 223 and 227.)

201 Healthy colour variations in the Tulip variety 'Gudoshnik'
Yellow, brown and reddish colours in a flame-shaped pattern could be considered a virus infection, but this particular variety has these colour variations when it is perfectly healthy.

202 Heat damage
This type of damage can occur when the bulbs are being given a hot water treatment for the control of stem nematode. If the temperature is too

high, or the bulbs are immersed for too long, the flower buds are damaged. However, no harm is done to the leaves and the following year the bulb will flower normally. The signs of this type of damage are small petals which are distorted and notched at the edge, while in very severe cases the whole flower is reduced to just a few millimetres of black growth.

203 Cucumber Mosaic Virus Disease

This disease is seen on the petals as narrow parallel stripes which are palest towards the tip of the petals and darker over the rest of the bloom. There is no real weakening of the tulip plant from this virus, but it is best to destroy any infected bulbs since this disease can infect a very large number of plant species, including members of the Cucumber (*Cucumis*) family and a wide variety of trees, bushes and herbaceous plants. Mezereon (*Daphne mezereum*) is often attacked in gardens (see no. 150).

204 Tulip Fire Disease, *Botrytis tulipae*

Initially developing on the leaves and flowers as small brown spots which elongate as growth continues, the disease eventually causes decay and rot of the tissues. On the outside scales of the bulbs the sclerotia, the bodies containing the resting spores, can be seen as hard, brown-black growths, about 2 mm in size. Sources of infection are from such bulbs, infected soil and from airborne spores from neighbouring diseased plants. The risk of spreading is always

highest under moist conditions. In the bulb the disease shows as a red-brown rot which is worst at the tip of the bulb. In addition to destroying all infected bulbs, spraying the growing plants during humid conditions with a suitable fungicide keeps the disease under control. Tulip fire does not spread to other plants.

205–206 Tulip 'Sports'

This appears to be a physiological trouble which makes the plant thin and weak with slightly pointed leaves and completely different petal colours. Whether the variety was originally yellow, red or pink, they all become light violet, pointed, and have a soft stalk. The precise cause is unknown since no actual disease or pest has ever been isolated. It is possible that it is a genetic mutation but how it occurs is unknown, particularly since sometimes the 'sport' is red or brown. All 'sport' plants should be destroyed.

207 Grey Bulb Rot, *Sclerotium tuliparum*

When the emerging shoot is about 5 mm high it can lose its usual green colour, stop growing, turn brown and die. This is due to grey bulb rot which is a fungus disease carried in the soil and not in the bulb. All infected bulbs must be destroyed and the soil should not be replanted with tulips or hyacinths for at least six years.

208 Mosaic Virus Disease

This disease appears on the leaves as long, yellow-green spots, but is rarely seen on the flower stalk and never on the bloom. Diagnosis should not be attempted on the lower part of the leaf as this is often discoloured on healthy plants. The symptoms show up best just before flowering. The disease causes steady deterioration in the growth and flowering of infected plants which should be completely destroyed.

209 Chocolate Spot

This virus disease shows itself as 2–5 cm-long spots of a dark chocolate colour near the tips of the leaves, and normally only after flowering. The plant can be weakened but it is not a serious disease, although it is best to remove infected plants.

210 Silver Leaf

This virus disease is neither common nor serious. It produces silver white to greyish stripes down the leaves after flowering and before the leaves begin to die down.

211 Blind buds

Blindness in the buds does not show up until just before flowering, when the buds fail to open and the outer sheaths become grey-white or brownish. The buds finally shrivel up completely and die back. This is not caused by any form of parasite but is purely physiological, due to unsatisfactory growing conditions. If these are improved, and particularly the supply of water to the roots, the plants will recover so that healthy flowers are produced the following year. Similar symptoms can occur in other bulbs, such as tulips, since they are all shallow rooting and very susceptible to drought and poor soil conditions.

212 Narcissus Fire Disease,
Botrytis narcissicola

In a mild attack the flowers are almost normal, but if the infection is severe the shoots are so weakened that the flowers are small and short-stemmed. On the leaves the fungus appears only on one side. This causes the leaves to twist and fall to the ground with a yellowy-brown discolouration along the diseased sides. The flower itself is rarely attacked. If the bulb is sliced longitudinally the internal brownish rot, worst towards the tip, is visible (see no. 214). In between the bulb scales the black resting spore bodies, or sclerotia, can be seen. Fire disease is the most serious disease of narcissus and is extremely difficult to control, even with repeated fungicide spraying. Infected plants are best removed and destroyed, and narcissus should not be planted in the soil again for about eight years. The disease only attacks narcissus.

213 Tarsonemid Bulb Mite,
Rhizoglyphus echinopus

This small, colourless mite, only half a millimetre long, is often found in large numbers in damaged or diseased bulbs. It makes the bulb soft to the touch and inside the tissue becomes brownish and powdery. Only firm healthy bulbs should be planted and soft bulbs should never be purchased.

214 Bulb Rot, *Fusarium oxysporum*

Bulb rot reduces leaf growth, which becomes thin and a verdigris-green, while flowering is poor. A longitudinal section of the bulb shows rotting which is most noticeable at the base of the bulb (see no. 212). Because the fungus can be carried in the soil it is advisable not to replant narcissus for a few years in soil from which diseased bulbs have been removed.

215 Grassiness (physiological)

The production of a large number of very slim leaves, giving an appearance of grass, and the complete lack of flowers are the typical symptoms of this physiological disorder. If the plant is dug up a large number of small bulbs are found, instead of the usual large one with two or three smaller ones. The exact cause of the disorder is unknown, it is possibly a genetic mutation since it is hereditary.

216 Stem Eelworm, *Ditylenchus dipsaci*

The eelworm is a microscopic round worm, also known as a nematode. This particular species lives in the bulb, but causes distortion of the aerial parts of the plant. The inside of the bulb has black rings which later rot, causing the bulb to become soft. It is another reason why only firm, hard bulbs should be purchased and planted. Infested plants must be removed and burnt, and bulbs should not be replanted in that soil for a number of years. This particular eelworm can live in the soil and also attacks a number of other plants. There is no chemical method of controlling an attack.

217 Large Narcissus Fly, *Merodon equestris*

This is another pest which causes the bulb to become soft, since its greyish, centimetre-long larva feeds in the centre of the bulb. Attacked bulbs will produce a few leaves but no flowers. The large, coarse flies are active at the beginning of the summer, laying their eggs in the soil around the bulbs. Some control can be obtained by using an insecticide around the bulb in June to kill the newly hatched larvae before they enter the bulb. Also make certain that only firm, healthy bulbs are planted.

218 Small Narcissus Fly, *Eumerus tuberculatus*

The larvae of this fly cause similar damage to that of the Large Narcissus Fly (no. 217), but whereas the latter only has one larva per bulb, this fly has several smaller ones in each bulb. The treatment is similar.

219 Heat damage on leaves

If the upper half or third of the leaves produce coarse, yellow-green spots it indicates that the bulb suffered from the heat treatment it was given during the previous resting period. The bulbs have not been permanently damaged, and will produce normal foliage the next year.

220 Heat damage in blooms

Distortion of the petals and corolla tube of the flowers is often caused by heat damage in a similar manner to the leaf damage (no. 219). Normal flowers will be produced the following year. The damage is caused by excessive heat during the bulbs' treatment with hot water to kill the stem eelworms.

221 Cold damage

A few centimetres above ground level the leaves may have a clearly defined belt of yellow, or yellowy-white. This actually occurred when the shoot was young and the temperature dropped below freezing for a short period, destroying the chlorophyll in the leaf tissue. No damage was caused, and the leaves will grow and function normally for the rest of the season.

222 Sparrow
The house sparrow, and sometimes the blackbird, will completely destroy the opening flowers of the crocus, probably in search of the vitamin A-rich saffron contained in the flowers. Yellow flowers seem to be preferred to other colours. Protecting the flowers is difficult if the birds are determined, bird scarers or chemical repellents can be tried but are not always successful.

223 Rattle
A virus disease recognisable by the strong yellow blotches, often a couple of centimetres in length, which develop on the leaves. The plants are weakened and the flowers become small. This virus will also attack tulips and hyacinths (see nos. 200 and 227). There is no control.

224 Mosaic Virus Disease
Small, yellow-green spots on the leaves are one symptom of this virus disease. Another, and more noticeable one, is the uneven discolouring and distortion of the flowers which never fully open. The infected plants should be removed and destroyed.

225 Bloom Stripe Virus Disease
In addition to the damage described in no. 224, virus disease can also be a striped discolouration of the flowers. Blue and blue-violet crocus blooms will change to blue-white or almost white. Again, infected plants should be removed and destroyed.

226 Zig-zag leaves
The zig-zag deformity of the leaves is quite distinctive and, in some years, fairly common. The flowers are produced normally. No pathological organism has been found in such plants, and therefore this damage appears to be purely physiological. It is probably due to frost or cold preventing the sheath enclosing the leaves opening quickly enough, to allow the expanding leaves to emerge. The deformity is noticed most in the yellow crocus but no permanent damage is caused to the corm.

227 Rattle
On hyacinths this virus disease develops as white-yellow stripes on the leaves, which later turn brown. The flowers become small and deformed. Infection may come from the bulb or the soil. Tulips and crocuses are also attacked by this virus (see nos. 200 and 223). Diseased bulbs must therefore be destroyed and susceptible plants should not be planted for a few years.

228 Soft Rot, *Xanthomonas hyacinthi*
Initially this bacterial disease causes very weak growth of the shoot, if it emerges at all, with yellow-brown stripes lengthways on the leaves. The leaves gradually become limp and rot. A cross section of the bulb reveals small, yellow, shining spots a few

minutes after the bulb has been cut. This is the most serious disease of hyacinths and since there is no treatment, infected bulbs should be destroyed and the surrounding soil sterilised or removed.

229   Mosaic Virus Disease

Infection with mosaic virus is indicated by a reduced number of buds on the flower stalk, faded or striped petals on the flowers and leaves with short, yellow-green stripes. The plants do not have the usual upright growth, the leaves turn over and fall, and the foliage starts to die earlier than on a healthy plant. There is no cure and infected bulbs should be destroyed.

230   Loose bud

When the flower bud is still enclosed by the leaves and close to the soil surface it can suddenly loosen and fall out. This unnatural growth is not caused by any organism but by unsuitable storing or growing conditions with variations in temperature and humidity. The bulb will probably develop normally the following year.

231   Green Capsid, *Lygus pabulinus*

Like other closely related insect species, the capsid bug feeds on plant juices, which can cause distortion and discolouring of the leaves and shoots. Flowering can also be delayed. The adults are brownish and about half a centimetre long. Their greenish, long-legged larvae or nymphs hide in between the leaves, but can be found by shaking the plant. The attack can be quite damaging around

mid-summer and the use of a suitable insecticide is often justified.

232   Earwig, *Forficula auricularia*

Dahlias are very attractive to this pest, which will often hide in the hollow stalk stumps at the base of the plant. They are rarely seen during the day, but at night they crawl up the plant and feed on the leaves and flowers, which can become quite tattered. When planting the tubers, all the old stalk stumps should be removed. An upturned flower pot with some sawdust under it will often attract the earwigs and avoid the necessity of having to spray with an insecticide.

233   Dahlia Smut, *Entyloma dahliae*

The fungus forms round, but later more irregular spots on the leaves. They vary in size from half to one centimetre across. Yellow at first, they become brownish later when the centre of the spot turns grey-brown. The disease is most prevalent where dahlias are grown continuously on the same soil. To control the disease either grow the dahlias on a fresh site, or spray a few times from June onwards with a recommended fungicide.

234   Mosaic Virus Disease

The disease shows as yellow-green variegations on the youngest leaves, which tend to remain stunted. The flowers become discoloured lengthways and assume a rumpled appearance. The whole plant is eventually stunted in its growth. There is no cure, so diseased plants should be destroyed.

235 Cabbage Moth, *Barathra brassicae*

In addition to feeding on plants of the cabbage family, the caterpillar of this moth also feeds on the leaves of dahlias and can also damage the buds. The moth, because of its bushy hairiness and large eyes, tends to resemble a miniature owl. It flies during July and August and lays its eggs on the leaves and petioles. The caterpillars can easily be collected because they are usually present singly. If too numerous for this they can be sprayed with an insecticide.

236 Mosaic Virus Disease

The first symptoms of the disease are yellow-green and yellow-brown discolourations of the leaves which lose their fresh green colour. Later, strong discolouration of the flower occurs, sometimes even when it is still in bud. There is no cure, so infected corms should be destroyed.

237 Gladiolus Thrips, *Taeniothrips simplex*

The adult thrip is black and, like its yellow larva, only a millimetre long. They feed on the surface of the leaves and flower petals, producing a whitish or silvery appearance on the eaten areas. They may even cause deformation of the flower petals. The adults usually overwinter in the corms, so these should be sprinkled with an insecticide when being stored, while the growing plants can be sprayed if treatment is considered essential.

238 Leaf Spot Disease, *Septoria gladioli*

Initially, it appears on the leaves as small, brown, round to slightly irregular spots, which will merge as they grow larger. Later, some small, black spore bodies form in the centre of the spots. An attack is usually worst in summers with long wet periods. Fungicide treatment is usually effective (see no. 239).

239 Hard Rot, *Septoria gladioli*

This is basically the same disease as Leaf Spot (no. 238), but affects the corms instead of the leaves. If the corm's outer dry scales are removed, the first symptoms appear as round, black spots but, as they grow, they cause the corm to dry up and go hard. Such corms should be destroyed in the spring before planting. Apparently the disease does not spread from the leaves to the corms or from the corms to the leaves in growing plants. Diseased material on the soil can overwinter and infect new plantings, so that after the disease has appeared gladioli should not be planted in the same ground for at least five years. Some control can be obtained by repeated fungicide spraying and good growth should be maintained in the plants.

240 Lily Beetle, *Crioceris lilii*

The bright red beetles emerge in the spring and commence feeding on the leaves of Lily (*Lilium*), Lily-of-the-Valley (*Convallaria*) and Imperial Crown (*Fritillaria*). The slug-like larvae continue to feed on the leaves throughout the summer, making them very full of holes. A closely related species, *Crioceris merdigera*, will cause very similar damage. If the beetles are too numerous to be hand collected an insecticide should be used at the beginning of May.

241 Lily Beetle, *Crioceris lilii*
See no. 240.

242 Mosaic Virus Disease
This virus develops as yellow-green, short broad stripes on the leaves, which are also produced much closer together on the stem, giving the whole plant a dwarfed appearance. There is no cure for the disease.

243 Anemone Rust, *Tranzschelia pruni-spinosae*
The fungus causes the leaves, particularly the oldest, to become reduced in size, a little thickened and covered with yellow-brown fungal growths, while, at the same time, flowering is reduced. In addition to Plum (*Prunus*), the fungus can also attack Wood Anemone (*Anemone nemorosa*) and will overwinter on De Caen (*Anemone coronaria*). Diseased plants should therefore be destroyed as fungicide spraying is ineffective.

244 Blind bud
In this physiological disorder the flower buds do not develop properly or emerge from the surrounding leaves. In most cases the buds dry up and become white or light brown (see no. 211), but in the anemone they turn black. Water starvation is the usual cause, and the plant will develop normally the following year if given sufficient water.

245 Cold damage
A few days after a sudden drop in temperature light brown sections appear on the leaves and they wilt. The damage is only temporary, leaves produced later are perfectly normal and often cover up the frosted leaves.

246 Leaf Miner, *Phytomyza minuscula*
The larvae of this fly can weave quite fantastic patterns of little tunnels in the leaves of aquilegia. The little maggots, only a few millimetres long, feed in the leaf between the upper and lower skin so that the leaf eventually wilts completely. Removal of attacked leaves may reduce the next year's attack, or an insecticide can be sprayed if it is considered essential.

247 Hollyhock Rust, *Puccinia malvacearum*
The rust is most apparent from spring until late summer. It appears as pale yellow, roundish spots on the upper surface of the leaves and larger growths, up to a couple of millimetres in size, on the lower leaf surface. On the leaf stalks and stems the disease shows as longish grooves which can be a black-brown colour as well as yellow. Because this rust does not have a host change, the spread of the disease can be minimised by cutting the plants down to ground level in the autumn and burning all the vegetation. Spraying with an anti-rust fungicide may also assist in limiting the attack.

248 Paeony Grey Mould, *Botrytis paeoniae*
The disease shows up just before the flower buds begin to emerge when the whole stem seems suddenly to wilt. All the growth then dies down. The cause of the trouble is at the base of the stalks where, close to the surface of the soil, there is a brown hollow section, often about 5 cm long, produced by the growth of the fungus.

The usual cause of the infection is very thick growth around the base of the plant obstructing air movement and increasing the humidity. The use of a fungicide is unnecessary if diseased material is removed and burnt and the remaining growth thinned out.

249 Mosaic Virus Disease

In delphiniums the disease produces yellow-green to yellow-white discolourations in fairly large sections of the leaves, particularly around the centre where the stalk joins the leaf. There is rarely any discolouration of the flowers, but they are fewer than normal and smaller. There is no treatment, so diseased plants should be dug up and destroyed.

250 Stem Eelworm, *Ditylenchus dipsaci*

This is the same nematode which attacks narcissus and other bulb plants (see no. 216), but in perennials it enters the stalks and leaves. The symptoms are particularly noticeable in phlox where the leaves become almost thread-like. Infested plants should be dug up and burnt, not placed on the compost heap. Susceptible plants should not be planted in infested soil for at least four years.

251 Leaf-eating Weevil, *Sitona lineata*

This and other *Sitona* species have acquired their name because of the manner in which they feed on the leaves. They make semi-circular cuts around the edges of the leaves of many members of the pea family and can be particularly troublesome in the early spring on seedlings. They

overwinter as adults under debris on the soil surface. They do little or no damage to large plants growing well, but seedlings may need treating with insecticide.

252 Leaf Spot Disease, *Septoria phlogis*

The circular leaf spots are red-violet, with a grey-white centre, and although they do grow larger they do not coalesce. The disease weakens the plants, but a couple of fungicide sprayings early in the summer usually control it.

253 Leaf Spot Disease, *Phyllosticta trollii*

On Globe Flower (*Trollius*) this disease produces leaf spots which in shape differ from most other forms of leaf spot. The young spots are grey-white to light brown in colour, but change to dark brown as the disease gets older. The plants are somewhat weakened, but the disease can be controlled by fungicide spraying during the summer.

254 Anemone Fire, *Tuburcinia anemones*

This is a fungus disease which causes blisters on the leaves and deforms them and the leaf stalks during their development. The blisters have a protective skin which is covered with a greyish layer of fungus at first, but later it bursts and the infected area becomes black. There is no treatment so diseased plants should be destroyed.

255 Christmas Rose Mildew, *Peronospora pulveracea*

In spite of the name, a real layer of mildew is seldom observed on the attacked leaves. The size of the leaves is reduced and the colour changes to a dull, grey-green. The number of flowers is also much less. This fungus overwinters in the rootstock, so that once a plant is infected it remains thus until destroyed. Since the most common method of propagating the Christmas Rose (*Helleborus niger*) is by dividing the rootstock, every care must be taken to use only healthy plants. Also, tools used on an infected plant can spread the disease so they should be dipped in disinfectant. If the disease is discovered in the first year the removal of infected leaves can stop it, otherwise the plant must be destroyed.

256 Leaf Spot, *Coniothyrium hellebori*

The leaf spots are 1–2 cm in width with clearly marked concentric circles and are a brown-black colour. Unless the spots occur in large numbers on a single plant no harm is done to the plant. If necessary a couple of fungicide sprayings can be made during the summer.

257 Leaf Miner, *Chylizosoma vittatum*

This leaf miner is responsible for the large, white-green mines, often partly filled with excreta, which are found on various plants of the Lily family (*Liliacae*). These include Solomon's Seal (*Polygonatum*), Lily-of-the-Valley (*Convallaria*), Hellebore (*Cephalanthera*) and Twayblade (*Listera*). The flies are active in the spring, lay their eggs on the lower surface of the leaves and the larvae commence to mine in the leaves, several to one mine. Attacked leaves can be removed and

burnt or the larvae can be squashed inside the leaf. If there are repeated attacks, an insecticide spraying in May is advisable.

258 Leaf Sawfly, *Phymatocera aterrima*

The 1 cm-long caterpillars of this common sawfly can often be seen on the leaves of Solomon's Seal (*Polygonatum*) and other closely related plants of the Lily family (*Liliacae*). The larvae are grey-green, broadest in front and with a brown spot on each joint. The damage may seem very considerable, but will suddenly cease some time in June when the larvae go into the pupal stage which overwinters. The black wasp, with smoke-coloured wings, emerges in May and lays its eggs on the lower surface of the leaves. If the attack is not too large the larvae can be hand collected, or alternatively an insecticide spray can be used as soon as the larvae are noticed.

259 Silver Y Moth, *Plusia gamma*

This is only one of several night-flying moths that can be seen in the garden. Others include the Cabbage Moth (*Barathra brassicae* (no. 235)), the Garden Noctuid (*Mamestra oleracea*) and the Pea Noctuid (*Mamestra pisi*). They are all a brownish colour with various discrete markings, hairy and of a similar size. They suck the nectar from various perennial flowers and lay their eggs on the stems and leaves. The caterpillars feed on the leaves and can cause considerable damage if present in large numbers. The chrysalis or pupa of the Silver Y is usually between leaves which have been spun together, but the other species pupate in the soil. Usually the larvae can be killed by hand, but if many moths have been seen and large numbers of caterpillars begin to appear an insecticide spraying can be justified.

260 Mosaic Virus Disease

In Bleeding Heart (*Dicentra*) the mosaic virus shows itself as very coarse leaf variegations. Reduced plant growth also occurs, but this is masked to some extent because of the early growth of the plant in spring and the fact that it dies down in late summer. Plants showing these symptoms should be destroyed.

261 Cuckoo Spit or Leaf Frog Hopper, *Philaenus spumarius*

The characteristic white foam or 'cuckoo spit' is usually deposited on the stem or in the leaf axil of many garden perennials. Inside is the green larva which feeds on the sap of the plant and secretes the foam for protection. Rarely are they present in sufficient numbers to justify any treatment.

262 Leaf Aphid, *Aphis sp.*

Several different species of aphids can attack perennials. Sometimes they are so numerous that they completely cover the upper shoots and leaves, crippling the plant by sucking its juices. In dry, warm weather their rate of reproduction is very high, they can become adult in less than two weeks and many are parthenogenetic, i.e. produce living young without fertilisation. They also secrete dew which becomes covered with the unsightly sooty mould fungus. The black 'fly' or aphid (*Aphis fabae*) is a species commonly found in gardens. The eggs overwinter on the Spindle tree (*Euonymus europaeus*), and hatch in the spring to a wingless generation. The winged generation which follows flies off to the summer host plants where, after several generations of wingless and winged aphids, a winged generation migrates back to the spindle tree in the autumn and lays the overwintering eggs. The Peach Aphid (*Myzus persicae*), another common species, can overwinter as the egg on peach and apricot trees or as the adult in glasshouses and beet stores. It is a major vector of virus diseases and is therefore a very serious pest. Plants suffering water stress are more susceptible to aphid damage than those that are well watered, so good watering in dry spells assists in their control. Insecticides should only be used early in the season since later the natural enemies will take over (see nos. 305–310) and the use of chemicals will kill them too.

263 Grey Mould, *Botrytis cinerea*

Although rarely found on the leaves, this disease can ruin the flowers of chrysanthemums, particularly if they are double or very dense. In warm humid conditions the fungus will develop a strong layer of greyish mould which will spread very rapidly, killing opened flowers and causing half-opened buds to rot. The disease attacks many plants and is the most common mould fungus on plants. During humid weather conditions susceptible plants should be sprayed with fungicide and all diseased flowers removed.

264 Leaf Miner, *Phytomyza atricornis*

This is one of the common species of leaf-mining flies which infests chrysanthemums and other herbaceous plants. The larvae are usually the cause of the characteristic winding tunnels in the leaves, although other *Phytomyza* species may be present also. They do not often cause sufficient damage to justify the use of an insecticide, infested leaves should be removed and burnt.

265 Turnip Moth, *Agrotis segetum*

The grey or green-brown caterpillars of this moth can reach 5 cm in length. They can cause damage to a wide range of plants by feeding on the leaves and the stems at ground level. They are known as 'cutworms' because of this feeding habit, as are the caterpillars of the related moths, the Heart and Dart Moth (*Agrotis exclamationis*) and the Large Yellow Underwing (*Noctua pronuba*). The moths fly at night and lay their eggs at the base of plants in June and July. The young caterpillars start feeding on the leaves, but soon go into the soil and then only come out and feed at night. These 'cutworms' are rarely present in sufficient numbers to cause much damage. Frequent cultivation and weed control keeps down their numbers, although insecticides can be used if necessary.

266 Grey Field Slug, *Agriolimax reticulatus*

Although the Grey Field Slug is the commonest of the garden slugs, the black Garden Slug (*Arion hortensis*) is also usually present. Slugs attack a very wide variety of plants, and by their method of feeding cause a tattering of the plant tissue rather than a clear-cut hole. They usually feed at night or after a period of rain when the humidity is high. Because they dry up if they have no moisture, slugs spend most of their time in moist soil, going deeper in dry weather. They lay heaps of translucent round eggs in moist places. Apart from their method of feeding, the presence of slugs is usually revealed by the slime they leave behind. They can be controlled by the use of ready-prepared slug bait which contains either metaldehyde or methiocarb, but treatment should be repeated every two or three weeks to deal with the young slugs emerging from the eggs.

267 Wood Snail, *Cepaea nemoralis*

Snails do very similar damage to slugs, their life cycle is the same and they can be controlled in the same manner (see no. 266). They are not so sensitive to moisture and can live under drier conditions.

268 Mosaic Virus Disease

The symptoms of the disease on Sweet Peas (*Lathyrus*) are yellowish variegations on the stems and a reduction in the colour of the flowers with some striping. There is no cure, and seed should not be taken from infected plants.

269 Thrips, *Thrips spp.*

The adults are a millimetre long, dark, slim and winged, while the larvae are yellowish and even smaller. They feed on the surface of the petals of many garden flowers, including asters, as well as on the leaves, causing whitish spots to develop on both. The insects usually hide among the petals and inside the buds. They can be found by shaking the plants over a piece of white paper. If an attack is very persistent an insecticide spray should be used.

270 Flea Beetle, *Phyllotreta spp.*
The worst damage done by these small, jumping beetles is to the seedlings of annual plants sown directly into flower beds. The small plants can be completely killed by the number of holes eaten in the young leaves. On larger plants the holes in the leaves do no real harm. The beetles prefer dry conditions, so well-watered seedlings often escape severe damage. Insecticide treatment can be used if necessary.

271 Thrips, *Thrips spp.*
These little insects can damage Marigolds (*Calendula*) just as severely as asters (no. 269). Insecticide treatment in May and June may be necessary to control them.

272 Powder Mildew, *Erysiphe cichoracearum*
The disease is rarely seen until late summer, when the plants have dense foliage. On Marigolds (*Calendula*) it deposits a greyish cover on the leaves but never on the blooms. This is a very common mildew since it attacks a wide variety of annuals and perennials in the garden. Although the plants may be a little weakened by the disease, its most important aspect is that it prevents them being used for cut flowers. If this is required fungicide spraying should start at the beginning of August.

273 Cabbage White Butterfly, *Pieris brassicae*
Whole colonies of the green variegated caterpillars of this butterfly can be found late in the summer on certain flowers. They are voracious feeders and can skeletonise the leaves on a plant without interfering with the flowering. There are two generations in the year, the first from May to July and the second from July onwards, and it is the second which does the most damage. The yellow, cone-shaped eggs can be found in clusters on the leaves during the time the butterflies are flying. When the caterpillars are fully grown they leave the plants and try to find a wall where they pupate, unless they have been attacked by parasites (see no. 300). Treatment with insecticide should be carried out when the caterpillars are small, as they are then easier to kill and have not caused any damage to the plants. The Small White Cabbage Butterfly (*Pieris rapae*) is rather similar, except that the caterpillars are not so large, the eggs are laid singly and they do less damage.

274 Sclerotinia Disease, *Sclerotinia sclerotiorum*
Too often this disease is not discovered until it is too late to prevent it spreading. Initially there is some soft tissue with scanty mycelium produced on the surface of the plant stalks. This is followed by the wilting of the leaves and flowers due to a reduction in the water and food supply to the top of the plant. If the stalk of a Sunflower (*Helianthus*) is sliced, the hard, black resting spore bodies of the fungus can be seen in the hollow pith. If

these fall to the soil they can remain viable for up to ten years. The disease may attack annuals, perennials and even soft-stemmed vegetables. Diseased plants must be dug up and burnt, there is no other treatment.

275 Root Rot Disease, *Pythium spp.*
The typical symptom of damage by these species of fungi is the contraction of the stem, or 'necking', just above soil level at any stage in the growth of the plant, but particularly in seedlings. Other fungi which live in the soil, such as *Rhizoctonia spp.*, can cause similar damage. This damage can cause the whole plant to wilt and die and is worst under damp conditions. If it is noticed early enough the use of a suitable fungicide may help, and if it is noticed every year in a certain area in the garden, the soil should be thoroughly treated with fungicide before further plants are placed there.

276 Mosaic Virus Disease
The mosaic virus of pelargoniums causes yellow-green leaf spots which can vary in shape from a ring formation to a continuous variegated area of undefined spots. Sometimes the yellow colouring is only present on the veins. The flower buds and flowers become reduced in number and size. There is no cure, and care should be taken only to take cuttings from completely healthy plants.

277 Pelargonium Rust, *Puccinia pelargonii zonalis*
The rust develops as pale-green to yellow-green spots with no clear outline on the upper surface of the leaf. On the lower surface corresponding grey-green spots are found, on which the brown-red spore bodies develop later. Treatment is difficult, although spraying with an anti-rust fungicide will help to control it.

278 Crown Gall Bacterial Disease, *Corynebacterium fascians*
This disease makes the pelargonium plant produce masses of small shoots sprouting in groups, either directly from the base of the stalk or close to it. They are light in colour and sometimes produce very small leaves, but development is not normal and growth ceases. The plants become weak, but rarely completely die. Infected plants should be destroyed and the soil sterilised, as there is no other treatment.

279 Iron deficiency
A deficiency of this trace element shows as yellow-green leaves which later turn yellow or completely white. At all stages the main and side veins stand out clearly as green stripes. The symptoms are most pronounced in the last leaves produced on a shoot. The deficiency is often induced by too much calcium in the soil, or the roots of the plant getting too close to the lime in a wall. Compost or freshly cut lawn cuttings dug into the soil will, over a period of time, improve the condition. However, a rapid improvement can be obtained by the use of a special iron chelate preparation which is applied to the soil.

280 Manganese deficiency

Manganese deficiency shows as a yellow-green discolouration on the leaves between the veins, starting from the outside edge and running inwards. The older leaves show the symptoms most. As with iron deficiency (no. 279), too much calcium in the soil often produces this deficiency, as it makes the manganese unavailable. It can be alleviated by using plenty of compost and keeping the soil moist, but a spray of manganese sulphate corrects the deficiency, or else a manganese chelate preparation can be applied to the soil.

281 Potash deficiency

When the edges of leaves turn brown, dry and curl inwards, the plant is usually suffering from potash deficiency. In severe cases the leaves will fall off. An excess of magnesium in the soil causes rather similar symptoms. Applications of sulphate of potash or nitrate of potash should be made to the soil, or for rapid results, the plants can be sprayed with a 1% solution of nitrate of potash.

282-284 Magnesium deficiency

No other mineral deficiency can produce such a wide variety of symptoms. At times there are yellow discolourations of the leaf edges which stretch down into the leaf between the veins, and sometimes these can become white. Sometimes there are brown, dead sections of the leaf between the side and main veins and this is often followed by leaf shedding. The deficiency can also show as red-violet colours following the edge of the leaf but a little way in. It

usually occurs in acid soils and a soil application of magnesium limestone will assist in the long run. For immediate remedial action spraying with 2% magnesium sulphate solution is best and this can be followed by a soil application of the same compound at the rate of 5 kg per 100 m².

285 Damage by wood preservatives on Privet
(*Ligustrum*)

Some wood preservatives will cause red discolourations, while others turn the plants white, yellow or brown. The damage usually occurs when the liquid drips directly onto plants, but it can also occur from the fumes of volatile preservatives some time after they have been used. The damaged parts will not get their proper colour back. When wood preservatives are used great care should be exercised in applying them and, if possible, adjacent plants should be covered with plastic.

286 Damage by wood preservatives on Tulips

Another example of the way in which wood preservatives can damage plants.

287 Hail damage on Lupins
(*Lupinus*)

Lupins have long flexible leaf stalks which give during a hail storm, so the damage appears as longish spots or stripes, or sometimes light brown, fairly round spots. The damage is usually worst on the side of the plant from which the storm has come (see no. 288).

288 Hail damage on short-stemmed leaf of a deciduous tree

When leaves have a short, rigid stem the hail stones go right through the leaf, and create irregular holes or give the leaf a tattered appearance.

289 Damage by weedkiller on Plane Tree (*Platanus*)

The leaves can be completely distorted with a yellow green appearance, thickened veins and a wrinkled leaf edge which may curl upwards. In addition to such damage being caused by spray or vapour drift when an adjacent area is being sprayed, it can also be caused by using an uncleaned spraying machine for another chemical after it has been used for weedkiller. It is therefore essential to thoroughly wash out any spraying apparatus, preferably with detergent, after it has been used for applying weedkiller.

290 Damage by weedkiller on Roses

Young leaves on rose bushes are very susceptible to weedkiller damage, either by spray or vapour drift. Older leaves and leaves produced after the damage are normally perfectly healthy. The plants will usually grow normally the following year.

291 Damage by weedkiller on Maple (*Acer*)

Upward air currents will sometimes carry spray or vapour drift from weedkillers well up into trees. The damaged leaves in the illustration were growing two metres above the ground. Again, thickened veins and a curling of the leaves are the symptoms of this damage (see nos. 289 and 290).

292 Short-tailed Field Mouse (Vole), *Microtus agrestis*

In spite of the name, the Field Mouse is not particularly attached to the fields but is found everywhere, particularly where there is dense grass, through which it makes its clearly defined runs leading either to its underground holes or to its feeding places. Most of its food consists of grass, and usually that at the base of the stems, so there is generally some debris left where it has been feeding. It can cause a lot of damage to trees and bushes by gnawing the bark, but because it cannot climb this damage is confined to the lower 10–15 cm of the trunks, where the small teeth marks can often be seen. Trees are often ringed by this gnawing which goes into the wood, and this can cause the death of the tree. Among the conifers the favourite trees are the Fir (*Abies*), Larch (*Larix*), Thuja, Dwarf Cypress or Thuja Cypress (*Chamaecyparis*) and Weymouth Fir (*Pinus strobus*). The adult field mouse is 10–13 cm long, with a 3–4.5 cm-long tail. The young are produced between March and September and there are 4–5 batches per season with 4–5 young each time. Where they are a serious pest they can be baited in their holes, trapped, or even gassed with a phosphate gas cartridge.

293 Red Mouse, *Clethrionomys glareolus*

The red mouse is a good climber so that during the winter it will gnaw the bark of trees quite high up. The damage is usually in a branch axil and continues from this point both up the tree and out on to the branch. In severe cases the trees can be completely stripped of bark and the buds are very often scooped out. This bud damage is particularly common on Fir (*Abies*) and Larch (*Larix*), and young trees which have been repeatedly attacked become bushy in their growth. The red mouse is only common in forest areas where it breeds from April to September having 3–4 batches with 3–5 young in each. The adult is 8–12 cm long with a tail of 4–7 cm. If they are so plentiful that they must be controlled, they can be killed with poison bait or caught in mouse traps using apple as a bait.

294 Mole, *Talpa europaea*

The mole digs more or less horizontal underground tunnels with slanting tunnels leading to the soil surface, and it is from these that the soil is pushed up to form the mole hills. During the warm summer nights the mole often leaves its system of tunnels to look for food above ground and then it always comes out through a mole hill. The hole can rarely be found because the mole closes it when it returns underground. The mole is very solitary and each system of tunnels is normally inhabited by only one mole. During mating and the raising of the young a pair normally live together, but this is the only time that they do. There is usually only one family each year, born during April or May and averaging four young. Moles need a lot of food and it consists mainly of earthworms, insects, millipedes, slugs and

snails, with some small vertebrate animals such as young frogs, baby mice, etc. Moles not only cause damage with their mole hills and shallow tunnels, but also by eating earthworms, although the number of injurious insects they eat partly compensates for this. The body of the mole is 12–15 cm long and the tail 2–3 cm. The fur varies from grey to a dark blue-black, although yellow specimens are not uncommon. Moles occur almost everywhere, and where they are too much of a nuisance they can be killed with the exhaust gases from a petrol engine or phosphene gas from special smoke cartridges. They can also be trapped, or poisoned with earthworms dipped in strychnine.

295 Water Rat, *Arvicola terrestris*

Although by preference usually associated with wet areas, the water rat can also thrive in dry situations. Wherever they are they dig a widespread system of deep tunnels. During the summer the holes leading to these tunnels can be easily found, the vegetation being chewed for quite a distance from them without any connection with the mound of soil. Water rats are entirely vegetarian. During the summer they live on the green parts of plants, eating them on certain definite places which become littered with debris and excreta. During the autumn they gather juicy pieces of roots and bulbs and store them in special larders connected to their underground tunnel system. In the winter they live on these but, in addition, feed on the roots of trees, bushes, etc., and it is because of this that they are considered a pest. The snout of the water rat is blunt, the legs short and the tail hairy. The adult is about 25 cm long, including the tail which is some 9 cm. Breeding time is April to November and there are four to five batches with about twenty young in all. The offspring can themselves breed at the age of two months. The water rat will not tolerate any related species on its territory, and the young are only allowed to stay on their mother's territory until they are about three weeks old. So, throughout the summer, the young water rats migrate to surrounding fields from any area inhabited by older ones. If necessary the water rat can be controlled by poison baiting or trapping, but they are rarely so numerous as to justify this.

296 Ichneumon or Sail Wasp, *Ophion sp.*

This fairly large wasp, nearly 2 cm long, belongs to the group of parasitic wasps which lay their eggs in the larvae of other insects. This particular one lays its eggs in the caterpillars of the Silver Y Moth (no. 259). These are slowly killed by the larvae of the wasp, although not until the parasitic larvae are ready to leave and pupate. There are a large number of these very useful wasp species, each being specific in respect of its host, and many contributing towards the control of insect pests.

297 Hunting Spider, *Tarentula pulverulenta*

This is one of the family of spiders that do not make a web in which to catch their prey, but rather lie in wait for them and then quickly pounce. The hunting spider is very efficient at catching flies and mosquitoes, but is unfortunately sensitive to many of the new insecticides.

298 Garden Spider, *Meta segmentata*

There are numerous species of web-making spiders in the garden in addition to this one, and they are all extremely useful in helping to control the many garden insect pests. They will catch and consume prey many times their own size, and the female is often so greedy that she will eat a male if he tries to mate when she is unready, unwilling or hungry.

299 Parasitic Wasp, *Ichneumon sp.*

This pretty centimetre-long parasitic wasp is one of many species that lay their eggs in the larvae of various moth species which serve as food for the wasps' larvae. Other wasps of the *Ichneumonidae* family live on beetles, aphids and even spiders, and many of them are not host specific.

300 Parasitic Wasp, *Apantales glomeratus*

This particular wasp belongs to the *Braconidae* family which chiefly parasitises butterfly caterpillars, although they are also found in aphids. When the larvae are fully grown they go into the pupal stage, either within the body of their dead host or in small cocoons which they spin themselves from a fine silk-like thread. This latter applies particularly to *Apantales glomeratus*, and most gardeners will have seen the dead cabbage white caterpillars almost covered by these small yellow cocoons. The small, black and very active wasps overwinter in the cocoons and emerge during the summer. Up to 150 wasp larvae can be found in one caterpillar and this parasite is the most effective natural control of the cabbage white butterfly.

301 Rove Beetle, *Staphylinus olens*

This particular beetle is one of the largest species of the *Staphylinidae* family of Rove beetles. The beetles are recognisable by their short, black wings and the long, narrow, very active larvae. Both feed on insects and small animals in the soil, and on dead vegetation and animals on the soil surface. They are very useful in assisting in the control of such soil pests as carrot fly, cabbage root fly and onion fly.

302 Carabid Beetle, *Carabus violaceus*

This is just one of the useful *Carabidae* family of beetles. The long-legged, big black beetles do not like the light and require dampness. They are therefore more active during the night or in dark places like cellars. The adults and larvae live on other insects, their eggs and larvae and are useful predators on aphids. Some species even eat slugs and snails.

303 Centipede, *Pachymerium ferrugineum*

Centipedes are usually an orangey-yellow colour and can be distinguished from millipedes by having only one pair of legs per segment. It is a very active predator, living on insects and worms in the upper layers of the soil, or on the moist soil surface at night. It bites and paralyses its prey with poison before consuming it.

They vary in size, the largest commonly found in gardens is 4 cm long.

304 Predaceous Capsid, *Anthocoris nemorum*

Although this little predator is only 3–4 mm long, it will attack and feed on much larger insects. It is particularly fond of spider mites but also feeds on scale insects and aphids. The adult overwinters under moss and leaves on the ground or in trees and comes out in the spring. Each female lays about 200 eggs and the nymphs, or larvae, of the new generation appear in June. Unfortunately they are very susceptible to insecticides and are one reason why the use of these should be kept to a minimum in the garden.

305 Parasitic Wasp, *Aphidius sp.*

These species are members of the *Ichneumonidae* (nos. 296 and 299), but are very small and only parasitise aphids. The eggs are laid actually in the aphids, and the larvae grow inside the host, without killing it, until they are mature and ready to pupate. This they do inside the mummified aphids and the adult wasp emerges by boring a small hole which is often visible in such dead aphids. There is considerable interest in the breeding of these small wasps for the biological control of aphids in glasshouses.

306 Hover Fly, *Syrphus balteatus*

Illustrated is of one of the large family of hover flies, many of which can be seen in the garden hovering over plants. They will suck a little nectar from the flowers and at the same time lay their eggs near colonies of aphids. As soon as the larvae hatch they start sucking the aphids, and these grey maggots can grow up to one centimetre long while clearing a leaf or twig of aphids. They fall to the ground to pupate and over-winter as pupae, although they usually have two generations in the year. It has been estimated that the larvae from one hover fly can, if they all survive, kill over two million aphids in the course of the two generations in a year.

307 Robber Fly, *Neoitamus cyanurus*

This long, narrow fly lies in wait for its prey between twigs or leaves (as illustrated), and catches other insects as they fly past. The larvae live near the surface of the soil and are also predaceous on other insects.

308 Lacewing, *Chrysopa carnea*

As its name indicates, the adult has lace-like wings over its green body which is about 1 cm long. It attaches its eggs with a very fine stalk to stems or leaves, usually the lower surfaces. When they hatch the larvae feed on aphids and small caterpillars, etc. The larvae have long legs, large heads and very strong mandibles with which to seize prey. The lacewing usually overwinters in sheds, lofts, glass-houses or similar sites. It has been estimated that the offspring of one female lacewing, if they all survived, would consume twenty million aphids in one season.

309 Parasitic Fly, *Dexiosoma caninum*

This species parasitises various beetle larvae in the soil. The fly lays its eggs on the surface of the soil and the newly hatched larvae seek out beetle larvae in the soil and work their way inside them. The fly larvae live in their hosts until they are fully grown the following summer, when they kill their host and pupate. One species, *Dexia rustica*, is specific in cockchafer larvae and may occur in as many as half the population of larvae.

310 Ladybird, *Coccinella septempunctata*

The red, seven-spotted species is probably the most common, but there are others with differing numbers of spots and there are also smaller, yellow ones with black spots. They all have typical, blue-green larvae which feed principally on aphids. There is only one generation a year, but the hundred or so larvae can consume some 130,000 aphids in their lifetime. The adults also feed on aphids. They overwinter under leaves and other debris on the soil surface, sometimes going into sheds and other shelters, but they can withstand the cold.

311 Titmouse or Blue Tit

The Tit family (*Paridae*) of birds are all active insect eaters and it has been estimated that one pair of tits will bring up to 16,000 insects to their young during a summer. They should be encouraged in gardens, since although they may appear to be damaging tree buds during the winter and spring they are actually only looking for insects and their eggs.

312 Hedgehog

One of the most useful animals in the garden, the hedgehog lives mainly on insects, slugs, snails and earthworms. It feeds at night and is rarely seen during the day. They can be encouraged to come into the garden if a saucer of bread and milk is put out each evening. They will overwinter in a quiet corner of the garden under a bed of moss and leaves.

313 Common Toad

Several species of toads can be found in gardens. They are all useful because their main food consists of slugs, worms and insects, many of which are harmful to plants. A few toads in a green-house can be quite useful at keeping the slugs under control.

APPENDIX

PESTICIDES

Pesticide Regulations

Pesticide regulations cover two aspects, the safety of the product and its biological efficiency. In those countries where there are statutory regulations and compulsory registration, the label must be approved by the relevant government authority before the product can be sold. The label will include the safety precautions which must be taken when handling and using the product, and the recommendations for use in accordance with the governmental and commercial biological testing.

In the U.S.A. the pesticide federal laws are administered by the Environmental Protection Agency, but the departments of agriculture in individual states are able to make variations in respect of biological recommendations according to their special conditions. In Canada it is the Pesticide Unit, Canada Department of Agriculture which administers the Pest Control Products Act. In Australia each state has its own laws, which in most cases are administered by the department of agriculture. In New Zealand the Agricultural Chemicals Board under the Department of Scientific and Industrial Research and the Department of Agriculture administer relevant legislation. South Africa has registration under the Bureau of Standards with the Department of Agriculture. In most countries the department of agriculture is involved in administering the regulations.

Among the major users of pesticides the U.K. is the only one with an agreed scheme between government and industry which is not mandatory. There are certain Acts concerning highly poisonous substances and, under the Farm and Garden Chemicals Act, the active ingredient must be stated on the label. The scheme is known as the Pesticides Safety Precautions Scheme (PSPS) and is operated by the Ministry of Agriculture, Fisheries & Food. All pesticides sold in the U.K. by reputable suppliers have been cleared through the Scheme and the labels contain a list of agreed precautions to safeguard users, consumers, the general public and wildlife. The precautions included on labels of registered products in other countries are very similar, in some cases the wording is identical.

There is no registration in the U.K. Instead there is the Agricultural

Chemicals Approval Scheme, again operated by the Ministry of Agriculture, Fisheries & Food, which is concerned with the biological efficiency of a product. All Approved products bear a large A and only products cleared under the PSPS can be Approved.

Gardeners should, therefore, only purchase and use products which have either been registered, Approved, or have the active ingredient, together with the precautions to be taken, clearly stated on the label. This latter will confirm that the product has been cleared in respect of mammalian toxicity, but has not necessarily been Approved for biological efficiency. Where registration is required there must be a registration number on the label.

Active ingredients of pesticides

Listed below are many of the chemicals used in fungicides, insecticides and other products in common use. It is not a complete list, but provides at least one for the chemical control of specific pests and diseases.

Bacteriacides and Fungicides

Antibiotics. Powder formulations. Effective against bacterial diseases such as fire blight of apples, thorns and pears.

Benomyl. Wettable powder formulations. Effective against many fungus diseases, including scab of crabapples, powdery mildew of ornamental plants and certain fungus diseases of turf grasses.

Captan. Effective against many fungus diseases, including black spot of roses and scab of firethorn.

Copper. Liquid and powder formulations. Effective against bacterial diseases and most fungus parasites that cause blights and leaf spots.

Dicloran. Wettable powder formulation. Effective against *Botrytis* fungi on ornamental plants.

Dinocap. Liquid formulation. Effective against powdery mildews of ornamental plants and many species of mites.

Ferbam. Wettable powder formulation. Effective against rust diseases, black spot of roses and many other fungus diseases.

Folpet. Wettable powder formulation. Effective against many fungus diseases of fruit and shade trees, black spot and powdery mildew of roses.

Maneb. Wettable powder formulation. Effective against leaf spot diseases of trees, rusts and black spot of roses.

Sulphur. Liquid and powder formulations. Effective against powdery mildews and also assists in the control of spider-mite infestations. Should not be used when air temperatures are above 85 degrees F.

Zineb. Powder formulations. Effective against the plane (*Platanus*) leaf disease and many other fungus diseases of trees and shrubs.

Insecticides and Miticides

Bacillus thuringiensis. This microbe, when used as an insecticide, will control many kinds of caterpillars.

Carbaryl. Wettable powder formulation. Effective against leaf miners, leaf beetles, lace bugs, the crawler stage of scales and earwigs.

Chlordane. Wettable powder and liquid formulations. Effective against soil-inhabiting pests such as ants, Japanese beetle grubs, chinch bugs, sod webworms, Taxus weevils and termites. Its use is restricted in some states.

Diazinon.* Wettable powder formulation. Effective against soil-inhabiting insects such as root worms and wire-worms, and leaf miners and white flies on ornamental plants.

Dicofol. Liquid and wettable powder formulations. Effective against many species of mites.

Dimethoate. Liquid and wettable powder formulations. A systemic insecticide effective against leaf miners, leafhoppers, sawfly caterpillars and mealy bugs on yews (*Taxus*).

Disulfoton. Powder and granule formulations. A systemic insecticide effective against sucking pests such as aphids, scales, white flies and mites when applied to the soil around ornamental and other non-edible plants.

Dormant Oils. Liquid formulations. Effective against many pests such as mites, mealy bugs, soft scales and some armored scales when applied to dormant deciduous and evergreen trees and shrubs just before new growth emerges in spring.

Lindane. Liquid formulation. Effective against aphids and lace bugs. In some states its use is restricted to trees for control of borers.

Malathion. Liquid and wettable powder formulations. Effective against sucking insects such as aphids, mealy bugs, boxwood psyllid, leaf miners and the crawler stage of scales. A premium grade of malathion sold as Cythion* has a lower odor content than the regular product.

Methoxychlor. Wettable powder formulation. Effective against tree borers, many leaf-chewing insects and the bark beetles that spread the fungus which causes the Dutch elm disease.

Pyrethrum. Liquid formulation. Effective against many small larvae but usually mixed with other insecticides to provide rapid knock-down effect.

Tetradifon. Wettable powder formulation. Effective against mites infesting ornamental plants.

Zectran.* Wettable powder and liquid formulation. Effective against many lepidopterous caterpillars, leaf miners, leafhoppers and many other insects infesting ornamental shrubs, vines and trees. It also controls snails, slugs, millipedes and sowbugs (pillbugs).

Metaldehyde and *Mesurol* (Methiocarb) are used in bait formulations for the control of slugs and snails.

APPROVED PESTICIDES IN THE U.S.A.

To provide American readers with a list of approved products available to them which are relevant to the text of this book, and to provide other readers with a guide, the trade names and manufacturers of these products are listed below:

Bacteriacides and Fungicides

Antibiotics
> Agrimycin, Merck, Sharp & Dohme
> Agristrep, Chas. Pfizer & Co.
> Phyto-actin, Pabst Laboratories

Benomyl
> Benlate and Tersan 1991, E. I. du Pont de Nemours & Co.

Captan
> Captan, Stauffer Chemical Co.
> Orthocide 50 W, Chevron Chemical Co.

Copper
> Bordow, Dow Chemical Co., Midland, Michigan
> Copper A, E. I. du Pont de Nemours & Co.

Dicloran
> Borran, Tuco Division of Upjohn Co.

Dinocap
> Karathane, Rohm and Haas Co.

Ferbam
> Fermate, E. I. du Pont de Nemours & Co.
> Niagara Carbamate, Niagara Chemical Corp., Division of FMC Corp.

Folpet

Ortho Rose & Garden Fungicide, Chevron Chemical Co.

Phaltan, Stauffer Chemical Co.

Maneb

Dithane M-22, Rohm & Haas Co.

Manzate, E. I. du Pont de Nemours & Co.

Zineb

Dithane Z-78, Rohm & Haas Co.

Parzate, E. I. du Pont de Nemours & Co.

Insecticides and Miticides

Bacillus thuringiensis

Biotrol, Thompson-Hayward Chemical Co.

Dipel, Abbott Laboratories

Thuricide HPC, International Minerals & Chemicals Corp.

Carbaryl

Sevin, Union Carbide Corp.

Chlordane

Velsicol Chemical Corp.

Diazinon*

Spectracide, Geigy Agricultural Chemical Co.

Dicofol

Kelthane, Rohm and Haas Co.

Dimethoate

Cygon, American Cyanamid Co.

Disulfoton

Di-Syston, Bay Chemical Co. (Chemagro)

Dormant Oils

B. G. Pratt Division of Gabriel Chemicals Ltd.

Lindane

Niagara Chemical Corp., Division of FMC Corp.

Malathion

American Cyanamid Co.

Cythion, American Cyanamid Co.

Methoxychlor

E. I. du Pont de Nemours & Co.

Pyrethrum

S. B. Penick and Co.

Tetradifon

Tedion, Niagara Chemical Corp., Division of FMC Corp.

Slug and Snail Pesticides
Metaldehyde
Slug-Kill, Plant Products Corp.
Snarol, Boyle·Midway Division of American Home Products
Mesurol*
Slug-Geta, Chevron Chemical Co.
Zectran*
Dow Chemical Co.

Animal Repellents
Deer and Rabbit Repellents
Chaperone Deer and Rabbit Repellent, Sudbury Laboratories
Repel, Leffingwell Chemical Co.

* Trade name

BIBLIOGRAPHY

Biological Methods in Crop Pest Control, George Ordish, Constable, 1967
Diseases and Pests of Ornamental Plants, P. P. Pirone, Ronald, 1970
Encyclopedia of Garden Plants and Flowers, Readers Digest, 1972
Garden Annuals and Bulbs, Anthony Huxley, Blandford, 1971
Garden Flowers, Eigel Kiaer, Blandford, 1972
Garden Shrubs & Trees, Eigel Kiaer, Blandford, 1973
Gardener's Bug Book, The, 4th ed., Cynthia Westcott, Doubleday, 1973
Pesticides and the Gardener, Royal Society for the Protection of Birds
Pest Recognition and Control for Amateurs, Keith M. Harris, 'Royal Horticultural Society Journal'. Vol. XCVII. Part 3
Plant Disease Handbook, rev. 3rd ed., Cynthia Westcott, Van Nostrand Reinhold, 1971
The Amateur Gardener, A. G. L. Hellyer, Collingridge, 1972

INDEX TO THE ILLUSTRATED SECTION

The illustrations and the descriptive text to them are indexed by both the English name and the Latin name where appropriate.

GENERAL INDEX